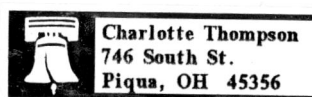

Charlotte Thompson
746 South St.
Piqua, OH 45356

D1794418

Spiritism in the Adventist Church

Colin D. Standish
President, Hartland Institute
Virginia, U.S.A.
and
Russell R. Standish
President-Director—Remnant Ministries
Melbourne, Australia

Published by
Hartland Publications
Rapidan, Virginia

Copyright © 1995 by C. D. Standish and R. R. Standish
All rights reserved
Printed in the United States of America

Hartland Publications
A Division of Hartland Institute
Box 1, Rapidan, Virginia 22733, USA

ISBN 0-923309-33-0

Spiritism in the Adventist Church

1. The Remnant — 5
2. Beware of False Shepherds — 14
3. The Origin of Spiritism — 20
4. Warnings of Spiritism in the Church — 27
5. Spiritism and the New Theology — 34
6. Adventists Begin to Waver on the State of the Dead — 38
7. The Bible Speaks — 43
8. The Resurrection and Immortality — 49
9. The Development of Spiritism in the Christian Church — 55
10. Minds Will Be Hypnotized — 59
11. Spiritism and Devil Possession — 66
12. Spiritism and the New Age — 73
13. Spiritism and Entertainment — 78
14. Spiritism and Doctrinal Deviations — 85
15. Seventh-day Adventist Publications — 92
16. Spiritism and the Health Work — 97
17. Spiritism and Celebration — 103
18. Spiritism and Witness — 111
19. Spiritism and Counseling — 115
20. Spiritism and NLP (Neuro-Linguistic Programming) — 121
21. The Way of Christ or the Way of the World — 129

1

The Remnant

In poignant language, the Lord spoke to Isaiah in his first vision—a vision of the remnant. It would be hard for any perceptive Seventh-day Adventist not to see that the tragic condition of Israel here described is paralleled by the state of the Seventh-day Adventist Church today.

> Hear, O heavens, and give ear, O earth: for the LORD hath spoken, I have nourished and brought up children, and they have rebelled against me. The ox knoweth his owner, and the ass his master's crib: but Israel doth not know, my people doth not consider (Isaiah 1:2–3).

Here the gospel prophet revealed that the Israel of his day, paralleling the Israel of today, had rebelled against the God of heaven. Such rebellion is always predicated upon a turning away from truth and righteousness. Though the "right" words are uttered, though the people go through the forms of worship, there is no power in them. The cry of the people is unheard by God because they have deviated from His truth and His righteousness.

> Ah sinful nation, a people laden with iniquity, a seed of evildoers, children that are corrupters: they have forsaken the LORD, they have provoked the Holy One of Israel unto anger, they are gone away backward (Isaiah 1:4).

There could hardly be a more vivid description of the state of the Seventh-day Adventist Church today. We are a sinful people, and we are laden with iniquity. On every hand we see, often even in high places, adultery, fornication, dishonesty, lying, ruthless treatment of our fellow members, embracing of false doctrines, and the inroads of satanic elements such as hypnosis and Spiritism. The prophet continues,

> The whole head is sick, and the whole heart faint. From the sole of the foot even unto the head there is no soundness in it; but wounds, and bruises, and putrifying sores: they have not been closed, neither bound up, neither mollified with oint-

ment. Your country is desolate, your cities are burned with fire: your land, strangers devour it in your presence, and it is desolate, as overthrown by strangers (Isaiah 1:5–7).

It has always been easy for God's people to admit that apostasy and ungodliness have existed in the past. It has also always been easy for them to recognize that the same apostasy and ungodliness may occur in the future. Rarely, however, have God's people, especially their leaders, had the courage and the honesty to admit that such frightful conditions exist in the contemporary church. The Seventh-day Adventist Church is no exception. There is the same deemphasis of the backslidden conditions in God's church. It is not difficult to get leaders or members to admit that there is some apostasy, but it is presented in a way that minimizes the depth and extent of that apostasy. Here is one typical example.

> No person acquainted with the Seventh-day Adventist Church would deny that throughout our history some apostasy has existed in our ranks and does even today
> (Roger Coon, *Tithe*, p. 3).

Presented in this way, it seems that today's apostasy is just a little like the apostasies of the past. Indeed, the apostasy in the Seventh-day Adventist Church today is so rampant and so extensive that myriads of our members are being swept into the final deception of Satan—Spiritism. Such mild statements as above are not meant to be honest before God in the presentation of the pervasiveness of the situation.

Let us continue reading Isaiah's presentation of the remnant.

> Except the LORD of hosts had left unto us a very small remnant, we should have been as Sodom, and we should have been like unto Gomorrah (Isaiah 1:9).

It is this faithful remnant that Isaiah most concentrates upon. If it were not for the remnant, Satan would have total control in the Seventh-day Adventist Church. This remnant, according to Isaiah, is very small. It is this small remnant that stands between Satan and the takeover of this world. Therefore, all his effort is thrust against this group. He has developed his masterpiece of deception in the vain hope that somehow, in this last moment in the history of this world, he will be able to destroy all of the faithful. It is the

Seventh-day Adventist Church, and the Seventh-day Adventist Church alone, that stands between Satan and the takeover of this world. If he could deceive every member of this church, there would be no final generation for Christ to take home to live with Him. Satan would be able to claim the undivided loyalty of the inhabitants of the world.

Large numbers of apostate members of the Seventh-day Adventist Church have not the slightest idea that their continued probation and the withholding of the judgments of God is due to the very group that they despise in the Seventh-day Adventist Church: those who truly

> keep the commandments of God, and the faith of Jesus
> (Revelation 14:12).

The Seventh-day Adventist Church is the only depositary of God's truth, and this is a truth that Satan hates with a passion. Therefore, he is concentrating his efforts at this time to deceive every member of the church. It is clear that only those who have daily surrendered totally to the power of Jesus Christ in their lives will be able to stand faithful amid the deceptions of the last days.

Unquestionably, God says to the Israel of today, as He said to Israel of old,

> Bring no more vain oblations; incense is an abomination unto me; the new moons and sabbaths, the calling of assemblies, I cannot away with; it is iniquity, even the solemn meeting. Your new moons and your appointed feasts my soul hateth: they are a trouble unto me; I am weary to bear them. And when ye spread forth your hands, I will hide mine eyes from you: yea, when ye make many prayers, I will not hear: your hands are full of blood (Isaiah 1:13–15).

We can hardly imagine the abomination to God that is the introduction of Pentecostal, New Age, and spiritualistic forms of worship in the Seventh-day Adventist Church. How nauseating it must be to Him to see His chosen people falling into the abominations of the wicked ones and pagans around them! Nevertheless, in spite of all this, Jesus is making a final appeal to His people.

> Wash you, make you clean; put away the evil of your doings from before mine eyes; cease to do evil; learn to do well; seek judgment, relieve the oppressed, judge the fatherless, plead for the widow (Isaiah 1:16–17).

With His love, He further calls us,

> Come now, and let us reason together, saith the LORD: though you sins be as scarlet, they shall be as white as snow; though they be red like crimson, they shall be as wool. If ye be willing and obedient, ye shall eat the good of the land
> (Isaiah 1:18–19).

This is the final call of Christ to His people today. It is the loving call of a God who, in spite of the apostasy of His people, is still making His loving entreaty to all who will turn from their wicked ways, and respond to the fullness of the power and the majesty of Jesus Christ in their lives. He also issues the warning to those who reject this final call,

> But if ye refuse and rebel, ye shall be devoured with the sword: for the mouth of the LORD hath spoken it (Isaiah 1:20).

Some may feel that the following words, as applied to the Israel of today, are too harsh, and hyperbolize the situation. For those who understand the extraordinary extent of the apostasy among the members of God's remnant church, however, these words are none too strong.

> How is the faithful city become an harlot! it was full of judgment [justice]; righteousness lodged in it; but now murderers
> (Isaiah 1:21).

Some might wonder why the term "murderers" would be used there. There have been in recent times a number of well-known cases of Seventh-day Adventists who have participated in premeditated murder; however, this is not what we believe the text to mean. Instead it refers to those who are leading men and women, not to earthly destruction, but eternal destruction. In that sense, false teachers and preachers are murderers of the worst order; for by misleading people, they rob them of their inheritance of an eternal home. There is no question that God places the condition of the church squarely to the account of those who have been given high leadership responsibility.

> Thy princes are rebellious, and companions of thieves: every one loveth gifts, and followeth after rewards: they judge not the fatherless, neither doth the cause of the widow come unto them (Isaiah 1:23).

The princes were the leaders of Israel. Of course, we must hasten to say that not every leader has fallen into this pathway. However, if the evidence can be properly evaluated, it would be fair to say that large numbers of those who have been chosen to be the leaders of God's remnant church have fallen into abject apostasy. They have been increasingly ruthless in their attempts to silence the voice of the faithful, feeble remnant. Many have become agents in the hands of Satan to intimidate and coerce those whose only goal is to be faithful to Jesus and to seek first the kingdom of God. Should we have any doubt that this prophecy concerning the remnant applies to God's people at the end of time? Paul puts the prophecy of the remnant in Isaiah 10:22–23 in an end-time setting.

> Esaias also crieth concerning Israel, Though the number of the children of Israel be as the sand of the sea, a remnant shall be saved (Romans 9:27).

Paul placed the prophecy as applied to the contemporary situation of Isaiah's time in the perspective of the final generation that will be left upon this earth. It is always hard for us as Seventh-day Adventists to apply this prophecy to ourselves; often we have sought to indicate that because we are "the remnant church," the vast majority of the members of other churches will fall and fail, but the members of the Seventh-day Adventist Church will continue to march heavenward. We usually give some vague acknowledgment that some will depart from the faith, but we are somehow moving into an era where most believe that God is too gracious to destroy the majority of His people. Israel of today is primarily the Seventh-day Adventist Church and it is evident from these prophecies that only a small number will be saved.

The authors of this book are burdened to awaken the consciences of laity and pastors alike to the sober reality of the state in which we find ourselves. If even a small number can be rescued from their headlong journey into eternal destruction by the shocking revelations of this book, that will be more than sufficient reward. Our only burden in writing so plainly and so outspokenly is to see souls preparing for the kingdom.

The identification of the final remnant is very clear. Only true Seventh-day Adventists can be part of the remnant. The Old Testament prophet, Zephaniah, clearly describes the remnant.

> The remnant of Israel shall not do iniquity, nor speak lies; neither shall a deceitful tongue be found in their mouth: for they shall feed and lie down, and none shall make them afraid
> (Zephaniah 3:13).

You will notice that the remnant people are those who have, through the power of the indwelling Christ, gained victory over every temptation. As they daily surrender their lives in earnest, soul-searching prayer to Christ to keep them from deception and from yielding to temptation, they are able to live a life wholly in accord with the will of God.

When there are so many who preach from our pulpits and teach in our schools the sin-and-live theology—that God's people will continue to sin until Jesus comes—we are developing a generation in which most accept that it is legalism or perfectionism to believe that victory over sin is possible. Satan has been able to twist the minds of Seventh-day Adventists, members of the church that began its pilgrimage towards the eternal home with the undying belief that

> Here is the patience of the saints: here are they that keep the commandments of God, and the faith of Jesus
> (Revelation 14:12).

This great church, which was founded upon the keeping of the commandments of God through the faith of Jesus, now is denying the very principles of its existence. The whole purpose of the emphasis upon the Sabbath truth was to restore the breach that had been made by most Christians in the commandments of God. Now, however, we have men attuned to the great lie of Satan, declaring to the members that it is impossible to keep the commandments of God. Such people will come confidently to the final climactic event—the return of Jesus. They will look up into the skies, expecting their eyes to be transformed to receive the immortality that God has promised, and suddenly they will realize that they are being destroyed by the brightness of His coming. It is impossible to anticipate or describe the anguish of soul and the desperation of this group of people, who have been thinking that they are heaven-bound, and now realize that they are lost for eternity.

Oh, what a responsibility rests upon the shepherds of the flocks, the pastors of the congregations, the teachers of our boys and girls and youth, to teach them the way of truth and righteousness! Tragic though it will be for anyone to be lost, how much more tragic for those who have led untold myriads into darkness and eternal destruction! It is important to notice the reverse side of Zephaniah's prophecy. If the remnant do no iniquity, then it is very clear that the vast majority in the Seventh-day Adventist Church will do iniquity. We may not have understood it this way, but clearly the statements of Christ toward the end of the Sermon on the Mount will apply to many Seventh-day Adventists.

> Many will say to me in that day, Lord, Lord, have we not prophesied in they name? and in thy name have cast out devils? and in thy name done many wonderful works? And then will I profess unto them, I never knew you: depart from me, ye that work iniquity (Matthew 7:22–23).

We must recognize that there will be many who have followed a pathway that seemed good, and have done things that in themselves were praiseworthy, but who did not fulfill the Biblical description of God's remnant's response to the tempter:

> And they overcame him by the blood of the Lamb, and by the word of their testimony; and they loved not their lives unto the death (Revelation 12:11).

What a tragic, agonizing scene this will be! In Revelation, John gives us further insights into the remnant.

> And the dragon [Satan: see Revelation 12:9] was wroth with the woman [church], and went to make war with the remnant of her seed, which keep the commandments of God, and have the testimony of Jesus Christ [the Spirit of Prophecy: see Revelation 19:10] (Revelation 12:17).

It will be noticed that in the New Testament, as in the Old, the "remnant" refers to those who keep the commandments of God: in other words, those who do not yield to temptation. They also have the Spirit of Prophecy. The reverse side says that the majority of Seventh-day Adventists will neither keep the commandments of God, nor will they, in the fullest sense of its meaning, have the Spirit of Prophecy. Is it any wonder that all sorts of efforts are being made to "make of none effect the Spirit of Prophecy" today?

Colin was preaching in Adelaide, Australia, some years ago, when a layman in deep agony said that his pastor had preached that it is "spiritual arrogance to believe that the Seventh-day Adventist Church is the remnant church. The remnant represents all people from all churches who follow the Lord." Then he asked Colin, "What can I say to my pastor?" Colin said, "Just ask your pastor what other church teaches men and women to keep the commandments of God, and what other church has the Spirit of Prophecy?" Reader, there can be no other church or message referred to than that of the Seventh-day Adventist Church. This is the only message that authentically fulfills these words of Scripture. However, as the vast majority of Seventh-day Adventists reject the very foundation and basis of the remnant, they too will go out into utter darkness while believing that they are imbibing of new and better light.

We must look at the reverse side of Revelation 12:17. The frightening revelation is that Satan is not making war on the entire Seventh-day Adventist Church; he attacks only the remnant. The reasons become very obvious on reflection. The majority of Seventh-day Adventists unwittingly are giving their lives and their ministries over to Satan. They are the best soldiers he has in his evil army. While professing to live in the light, they are agents of darkness. He does not make war upon them; they are the saboteurs, the traitors of the cause of Jesus Christ, and instead of leading men and women to the light of God's truth, they are leading them to the darkness of destruction.

As we explore the condition of our beloved church in this book, it is essential that our emotions be not those of anger, hatred, bitterness, or animosity, but of heart-felt love, deep concern and sorrow for the state of our church. We must have a burden for the souls that have within their grasp the depositories of God's truth, yet who have been blinded by the prince of this world. The Lord gives a sobering call to each one of us.

> Men of action are needed—men who will labor with earnest, ceaseless energy for the purifying of the church and the warning of the world (*Testimonies for the Church*, vol. 5, p. 187).

This is the call to every earnest, dedicated Seventh-day Adventist today. This remnant will not be destroyed by Satan. It will stand in Christ's strength between Satan and the takeover of the world. This is the remnant that is referred to in the Scriptures as the gold, the sheep, the wheat. A unity will come that is built upon a truth that sanctifies (John 17:17). This is the remnant of which Peter speaks,

> Seeing ye have purified your souls in obeying the truth through the Spirit unto unfeigned love of the brethren, see that ye love one another with a pure heart fervently: being born again, not of corruptible seed, but of incorruptible, by the word of God, which liveth and abideth for ever (1 Peter 1:22–23).

2

Beware of False Shepherds

The prophet, Jeremiah presents in vivid and startling terms the condition of God's people. As it was with the prophet Isaiah's warnings, Jeremiah's messages are more relevant for us today than even for the day in which he lived.

> Lift up thine eyes unto the high places, and see where thou hast not been lien with. In the ways hast thou sat for them, as the Arabian in the wilderness; and thou hast polluted the land with thy whoredoms and with thy wickedness. Therefore the showers have been withholden, and there hath been no latter rain; and thou hadst a whore's forehead, thou refusedst to be ashamed (Jeremiah 3:2–3).

This startling description of the state of God's church is hard for us to accept. The cries of peace and safety are to be heard everywhere. The tragedy is that these cries come mainly from the ministry. Ellen White warns us,

> Shake off your spiritual lethargy. Work with all your might to save your own souls and the souls of others. It is no time now to cry peace and safety. It is not silver-tongued orators that are needed to give this message. The truth in all its pointed severity must be spoken
> (*Testimonies for the Church*, vol. 5, p. 187).

We have often used this "peace and safety" message to talk about conditions in the political world, such as the cry that there will be no more war. Never once does Sister White use it in this context, though. In her writings, the "peace and safety" deception is always associated with unfaithful ministers lulling the congregations into carnal security.

> Those who are at ease in Zion cry peace and safety, while Heaven declares that swift destruction is about to come upon the transgressor. The young, the frivolous, the pleasure loving, consider these warnings as idle tales, and turn from them with a jest. Parents are inclined to think their children about

right in the matter, and all sleep on at ease. Thus it was at the destruction of the old world, and when Sodom and Gomorrah were consumed by fire
(Testimonies for the Church, vol. 5, p. 233).

We are near the close of time. I have been shown that the retributive judgments of God are already in the land. The Lord has given us warning of the events about to take place. Light is shining from his word, yet darkness covers the earth, and gross darkness the people. "While they shall cry, Peace and safety; sudden destruction cometh upon them, . . . and they shall not escape"
(Testimonies for the Church, vol. 5, p. 99).

But too often the leader has stood hesitating, seeming to say: "Let us not be in too great haste. There may be a mistake. We must be careful not to raise a false alarm." The very hesitancy and uncertainty on his part is crying; "Peace and safety"
(Testimonies for the Church, vol. 5, p. 715).

Sister White describes the terrible judgments that will fall upon pastors and leaders who merely try to calm the concerns of the laity.

Here we see that the church—the Lord's sanctuary—was the first to feel the stroke of the wrath of God. The ancient men, those to whom God had given great light, and who had stood as guardians of the spiritual interests of the people, had betrayed their trust. They had taken the position that we need not look for miracles and the marked manifestation of God's power as in former days. Times have changed. These words strengthen their unbelief, and they say, The Lord will not do good, neither will he do evil. He is too merciful to visit His people in judgment. Thus peace and safety is the cry from men who will never again lift up their voice like a trumpet to show God's people their transgressions and the house of Jacob their sins. These dumb dogs that would not bark, are the ones who feel the just vengeance of an offended God. Men, maidens, and little children, all perish together
(Testimonies for the Church, vol. 5, p. 211).

Surely, this is the time when every chosen pastor of the Lord must

> Cry aloud, spare not, lift up thy voice like a trumpet, and shew my people their transgression, and the house of Jacob their sins (Isaiah 58:1).

We must repeat the words of Isaiah,

> For Zion's sake will I not hold my peace, and for Jerusalem's sake I will not rest, until the righteousness thereof go forth as brightness, and the salvation thereof as a lamp that burneth (Isaiah 62:1).

Now is the time for every leader and minister to recognize that

> I [God] have set thee a watchman unto the house of Israel; therefore thou shalt hear the word at my mouth, and warn them from me. When I say unto the wicked, O wicked man, thou shalt surely die; if thou dost not speak to warn the wicked from his way, that wicked man shall die in his iniquity; but his blood will I require at thine hand. Nevertheless, if thou warn the wicked of his way to turn from it; if he do not turn from his way, he shall die in his iniquity; but thou hast delivered thy soul (Ezekiel 33:7–9).

Those leaders, pastors, and teachers who believe that it is love and kindness that prompts them to comfort men and women in their sin have no true love for souls. Too often the motivation is a desire to be pleasing and to receive flattery. If we have a love for souls and an earnestness for the kingdom of God, we cannot hold our peace in this time of almost unbridled apostasy and wickedness in our church.

There is a grave warning to laity not to follow men, but to put their trust only in God and His Word. The leaders and pastors are not the only ones who have become men-pleasers; a servile laity is following the words of man and ignoring and rejecting the words of God. The warnings are fearful concerning the shepherds that lead God's people astray.

> Woe be unto the pastors that destroy and scatter the sheep of my pasture! saith the LORD. Therefore thus saith the LORD God of Israel against the pastors that feed my people; Ye have scattered my flock, and driven them away, and have not visited them: behold, I will visit upon you the evil of your doings, saith the LORD (Jeremiah 23:1–2).

> My people hath been lost sheep: their shepherds have caused them to go astray, they have turned them away on the mountains: they have gone from mountain to hill, they have forgotten their restingplace (Jeremiah 50:6).

> Son of man, prophesy against the shepherds of Israel, prophesy, and say unto them, Thus saith the Lord God unto the shepherds; Woe be to the shepherds of Israel that do feed themselves! should not the shepherds feed the flocks? (Ezekiel 34:2)

> Therefore, O ye shepherds, hear the word of the LORD; Thus saith the Lord God; Behold, I am against the shepherds; and I will require my flock at their hand, and cause them to cease from feeding the flock; neither shall the shepherds feed themselves any more; for I will deliver my flock from their mouth, that they may not be meat for them (Ezekiel 34:9–10).

Some find it difficult to associate such texts with the circumstances that exist in God's church today. However such circumstances existed even in the apostolic times, and Satan, in his final effort to derail the Seventh-day Adventist Church from its mission and destiny, has certainly been no less vigilant in these last days.

Paul put it this way,

> But there be some that trouble you, and would pervert the gospel of Christ (Galatians 1:7).

Furthermore, Paul's moving charge to the church at Ephesus surely applies to us today.

> Take heed therefore unto yourselves, and to all the flock, over the which the Holy Ghost hath made you overseers, to feed the church of God, which he hath purchased with his own blood. For I know this, that after my departing shall grievous wolves enter in among you, not sparing the flock. Also of your own selves shall men arise, speaking perverse things, to draw away disciples after them (Acts 20:28–30).

The same challenges come today as we see men claiming to be the ministers of Christ who are leading astray the precious flock that God has entrusted to them. The deception is always built upon the sin-and-live theology, on the perversion of the messages on the Investigative Judgment and the sanctuary, and on carelessness about Christian lifestyle and standards, all in the name of the gospel. It was against such an antinomian gospel that Jude warned when he said,

> For there are certain men crept in unawares, who were before of old ordained to this condemnation, ungodly men, turning the grace of our God into lasciviousness, and denying the only Lord God, and our Lord Jesus Christ (Jude 4).

However, there is great consolation in the Word of God. God will not allow His people always to be trodden down by unfaithful shepherds. He has promised that He will restore them.

> And I will gather the remnant of my flock out of all countries whither I have driven them, and will bring them again to their folds; and they shall be fruitful and increase. And I will set up shepherds over them which shall feed them: and they shall fear no more, nor be dismayed, neither shall they be lacking, saith the LORD (Jeremiah 23:3–4).

> For thus saith the Lord GOD; Behold, I, even I, will both search my sheep, and seek them out. As a shepherd seeketh out his flock in the day that he is among his sheep that are scattered; so will I seek out my sheep, and will deliver them out of all places where they have been scattered in the cloudy and dark day. And I will bring them out from the people, and gather them from the countries, and will bring them to their own land, and feed them upon the mountains of Israel by the rivers, and in all the inhabited places of the country. I will feed them in a good pasture, and upon the high mountains of Israel shall their fold be: there shall they lie in a good fold, and in a fat pasture shall they feed upon the mountains of Israel. I will feed my flock, and I will cause them to lie down, saith the Lord GOD. I will seek that which was lost, and bring again that which was driven away, and will bind up that which was broken, and will strengthen that which was sick: but I will destroy the fat and the strong; I will feed them with judgment (Ezekiel 34:11–16).

> I will gather them that are sorrowful for the solemn assembly, who are of thee, to whom the reproach of it was a burden. Behold, at that time I will undo all that afflict thee: and I will save her that halteth, and gather her that was driven out; and I will get them praise and fame in every land where they have

been put to shame. At that time will I bring you again, even in the time that I gather you: for I will make you a name and a praise among all people of the earth, when I turn back your captivity before your eyes, saith the Lord

(Zephaniah 3:18–20).

How wonderful is our God! In spite of the persecution and the furor of unfaithful people, God has promised to bring His people back and to honor them before all the nations of the world. This is not a time for God's people to become discouraged, for discouragement is of Satan. This is not a time to be silent. God's people must now rise up as never before, recognizing that their redemption draweth nigh, and that the Lord is their strength and stay. He is the One Who will reward according as our works may be.

The remnant have a God-given responsibility to do everything possible to win to the fold of truth those who know it not, whether they be in the church or the world. As apostasy floods into the church, God's remnant will not waver, nor will they be intimidated. They will represent those who will not be bought or sold, that cannot be bribed, flattered or threatened away from God's truth. They are men and women who lean fully and completely on the power of Jesus in their lives every day. This call for loyalty resounds with greater authenticity every moment that we draw closer to the end of time.

3

The Origin of Spiritism

The prophet, Ezekiel gives a vivid description of the first evidence of iniquity in the universe. From eternity one pulsation of harmony had reigned. The whole law of every being had always been the law of selflessness, the law of giving. However, one allowed the canker of sin to well up in his own life and, like all other apostates, he wanted to share it. These are Ezekiel's words:

> Thou art the anointed cherub that covereth; and I have set thee so: thou wast upon the holy mountain of God; thou hast walked up and down in the midst of the stones of fire. Thou wast perfect in thy ways from the day that thou wast created, till iniquity was found in thee.... Thine heart was lifted up because of thy beauty, thou hast corrupted thy wisdom by reason of thy brightness: I will cast thee to the ground, I will lay thee before kings, that they may behold thee
> (Ezekiel 28:14–15, 17).

Isaiah too gave a graphic account of the fall of Lucifer.

> How art thou fallen from heaven, O Lucifer, son of the morning! how art thou cut down to the ground, which didst weaken the nations! For thou hast said in thine heart, I will ascend into heaven, I will exalt my throne above the stars of God: I will sit also upon the mount of the congregation, in the sides of the north: I will ascend above the heights of the clouds; I will be like the most High (Isaiah 14:12–14).

Jesus described the satanic deception in the lives of those who are unfaithful to the Lord:

> Ye are of your father the devil, and the lusts of your father ye will do. He was a murderer from the beginning, and abode not in the truth, because there is no truth in him. When he speaketh a lie, he speaketh of his own: for he is a liar, and the father of it (John 8:44).

John had this to say:

> He that committeth sin is of the devil; for the devil sinneth from the beginning. For this purpose the Son of God was manifested, that he might destroy the works of the devil
> (1 John 3:8).

Every sin that has ever been committed in the universe has had its origin with Satan. It has ever been his purpose to win the loyalty of every being. In heaven he won the loyalty of one-third of the angels. His success has been vastly greater upon the earth. Never has there been more than a small percentage of the world's population that have given their loyalty to God. The basis of every satanic thrust is the issue of lies. The battle is not the battle between truth and error, but between truth on the one hand and the mixture of truth and error on the other. In the Garden of Eden it was not the Tree of the Knowledge of Evil that caused the fall of our earthly parents, it was the Tree of the Knowledge of Good—and Evil. So down the ages Satan has mixed truth and error in varying proportions with one purpose in mind—to lead men and women with him into eternal destruction.

The first deception of Satan involved Spiritism. Moses described how the serpent was used as a spiritualistic medium (Genesis 3:1–5). There was only one purpose, and that was to destroy confidence in the Word of God. That has always been the purpose of Spiritism: to lead men from following the pathway of God's truth into the pathway of unrighteousness. Adam and Eve had the choice that every human being subsequently has had to make—whether to accept the word of the One Who is the Truth (John 14:6), Who cannot lie (Titus 1:2); or to accept the word of the one who is the father of lies (John 8:44).

At the end of time, Satan is desperately accelerating his efforts to deceive the whole world. John expressed it this way:

> The devil is come down unto you, having great wrath, because he knoweth that he hath but a short time
> (Revelation 12:12).

Speaking of Satan's assault on the youth, Peter said,

> Be sober, be vigilant; because your adversary the devil, as a roaring lion, walketh about, seeking whom he may devour
> (1 Peter 5:8).

The fury of Satan is directed against God's faithful people. When the disciples came to Jesus and questioned Him about the shocking prediction that Jerusalem would be destroyed and the temple dismantled, they asked Him the question,

> Tell us, when shall these things be? and what shall be the sign of thy coming, and of the end of the world?
> (Matthew 24:3).

Often we overlook the very first, and probably the greatest, sign that Jesus is coming soon. The answer was given in verse four.

> Take heed that no man deceive you (Matthew 24:4).

Believable and—outside of the power of the indwelling Christ—irresistible deceptions will come upon the world. Expounding a little later, Jesus said,

> For there shall arise false Christs, and false prophets, and shall shew great signs and wonders; insomuch that, if it were possible, they shall deceive the very elect (Matthew 24:24).

It is obvious that Satan's greatest assault is upon the very elect, for they are the ones who stand between him and the deception of the whole world. Much of this work will be done by the emissaries of Satan, but he himself will also work against them.

> For such are false apostles, deceitful workers, transforming themselves into the apostles of Christ. And no marvel; for Satan himself is transformed into an angel of light. Therefore it is no great thing if his ministers also be transformed as the ministers of righteousness; whose end shall be according to their works (2 Corinthians 11:13–15).

There are many statements in the writings of Sister White which confirm the centrality of Spiritism that will take over the world at the end of time.

> The condition of society today is the same as when God presented before Israel the abominations of the heathen; and the same warnings are necessary to the remnant people. Spiritualism is advancing through the land in triumph. "The spirits of devils working miracles" are going "forth unto the kings of the earth and of the whole world, to gather them to the battle of the great day of God Almighty." Men are seeking unto

them that have familiar spirits; but the people of God cannot in any sense follow the practices of the world. They must keep the commandments of the Lord. The line of separation must be distinctly marked between the obedient and the disobedient. There must be open and avowed enmity between the church and the serpent, between her seed and his seed
(*Signs of the Times*, August 26, 1889).

We must keep in mind that all in the world are going to turn to the Papacy except those whose names are enshrined in the Lamb's Book of Life.

And all that dwell upon the earth shall worship him, whose names are not written in the book of life of the Lamb slain from the foundation of the world (Revelation 13:8).

It is no doubt by Spiritism and its associate art of hypnotism that Satan will bring all unconverted hearts into apparent unity. This Spiritism is, of course, not new. As we have seen, it was found in the Garden of Eden when Satan used the serpent to deceive Eve. Throughout the history of the world, Spiritism has been used constantly to deceive mankind.

The warnings of the word of God regarding the perils surrounding the Christian church belong to us today. As in the days of the apostles men tried by tradition and philosophy to destroy faith in the Scriptures, so today, by the pleasing sentiments of "higher criticism," evolution, Spiritualism, theosophy, and pantheism, the enemy of righteousness is seeking to lead souls into forbidden paths. To many, the Bible is as a lamp without oil, because they have turned their minds into channels of speculative belief that bring misunderstanding and confusion. The work of "higher criticism," in dissecting, conjecturing, reconstructing, is destroying faith in the Bible as a divine revelation. It is robbing God's word of power to control, uplift, and inspire human lives. By Spiritualism, multitudes are taught to believe that desire is the highest law, that license is liberty, and that man is accountable only to himself
(*Acts of the Apostles,* p. 474).

Sister White makes many statements pointing out that false doctrines and beliefs, as well as worldly and self-centered practices, are the result of Spiritism. When we see how thoroughly such theories and practices are taking over the philosophy of the world, we can understand that already Spiritism has made great inroads into our planet. The majority of its inhabitants may even now be under the satanic control of Spiritism.

> The magicians of heathen times have their counterpart in the spiritualistic mediums, the clairvoyants, and the fortune-tellers of today. The mystic voices that spoke at Endor and at Ephesus are still by their lying words misleading the children of men. Could the veil be lifted from before our eyes, we should see evil angels employing all their arts to deceive and to destroy. Wherever an influence is exerted to cause men to forget God, there Satan is exercising his bewitching power. When men yield to his influence, ere they are aware the mind is bewildered and the soul polluted. The apostle's admonition to the Ephesian church should be heeded by the people of God today: "Have no fellowship with the unfruitful works of darkness, but rather reprove them" (*Acts of the Apostles,* p. 290).

It is only natural that as spiritualistic principles pervade the world, they will make an enormous impact upon our beloved Seventh-day Adventist Church. We cannot find any evidence in the Scriptures that there is a natural protection around those who claim to be part of the body of Jesus Christ. Indeed, on the contrary, Scripture calls constantly for a total commitment to Christ as the only safeguard against the satanic thrusts that have always been present. Christ affirmed,

> Without me ye can do nothing (John 15:5).

With all the clear testimony that God has given to us on this issue, each member of the church must be fully alert to the wily efforts of Satan today to bring every human being under his banner. Knowing that Christ, through the Seventh-day Adventist Church, alone stands between him and the takeover of this world, Satan is seeking to undermine every church member, thus destroying their eternal inheritance. Only day-by-day vigilance and total surrender of the life to Christ can keep us from being deceived by Satan.

Whereas once Christian nations eschewed witchcraft and its concomitant manifestations, today in America it has all but been declared a religion, protected under the First Amendment of the Constitution. This is in spite of the fact that the First Amendment has been eroded dramatically in recent times. Declared witches have been granted time off work to celebrate their religious holidays. A woman who was dismissed from employment by the Salvation Army because she was photocopying satanic material was ruled by the courts to have been unlawfully dismissed. The Salvation Army was the recipient of federal funding for the project on which this woman was working, and therefore the court ruled that the Salvation Army could not discriminate against her.

The impact of spiritualism in New Age is indicated over and over again. *Time* magazine's November 4, 1991 cover story was entitled, "The New Age of Alternative Medicine." It divided the various forms of such medicine in four categories:

(1) *Botanical,* which includes Aromatherapy (the use of essential oils from plants and flowers to massage into the skin or to inhale), Medicinal Herbalism (promoting health and treating illness with plant-derived potions), and Homeopathy (the use of minute quantities of remedies that in larger doses produce effects similar to those of the disease being treated).

(2) *Lifestyle New Age Approaches,* which includes Macrobiotics (dietary and health discipline based on balancing yin [passive energy] and yang [active energy] (this balancing of yin and yang comes directly from Chinese paganism), Ayurvedic medicine (a four-thousand-year-old Indian system in which diet and therapies—mostly herbs and massage—depend on body type), and Holistic medicine (a variation on conventional medicine that emphasizes lifestyle and psychological factors by treating the whole person).

(3) *Manipulative Hands-on,* which includes Reflexology (massaging areas of the feet to affect the rest of the body), Rolfing (deep and sometimes painful massage to realign the body), Shiatsu (Japanese therapeutic massage using pressure points), Alexander technique (training to improve poor posture and thereby alleviate pain), Chiropractic (manipulation of the spine to relieve backache and other ailments), Acupressure (using fingers instead of needles in a technique similar to acupuncture), and Acupuncture (a two-

thousand-year old Chinese method of easing pain and maintaining health by inserting fine needles into the body at specific points that relate to different parts of the body).

(4) *Mind Over Matter,* which includes Color healing (shining colored lights on the body to alter the vibration aura), Crystal healing (a New Age therapy purporting to derive healing energy from quartz and other minerals), Bioenergetics (exchange of "energy" between patient and therapist), Guided Imagery (therapy in which patients are encouraged to envisage their own immune systems battling disease), Hypnotherapy (making therapeutic suggestions to patients who are in a semi-conscious trance to relieve pain and speed healing), and Biofeedback (use of machines to train people to control such involuntary functions as jaw tension, heart rate and circulation in the hands).

This Time magazine article gave the reason why New Age medicine is becoming popular. Many people, fed up with allopathic medicine, are turning to alternative methods. Rather than using the simple, natural remedies that God has given to alleviate sickness and to restore health, they are moving into the mystical and the pagan. While there may be some elements of good in some of these therapies, each one of them has its roots in mysticism, paganism, and in what now has been brought together in one conjunction of paganism, Spiritism and humanism: the New Age.[1]

We have reached the point where almost every publicly advertised enhancement-type seminar is under the control of New Age theories and philosophies. Extraordinary care needs to be exercised when considering attending and funding such programs as stress control, marriage enhancement, leadership, salesmanship, mind expansion, educational improvement, enhanced interpersonal relations, and similar seminars. What may at first seem good or desirable will probably turn out to be a program built on spiritualistic and pagan principles.

Surely this is a time for special spiritual guidance in the lives of all of God's people, and alertness to the unbelievable dangers that are testing the loyalty of God's end-time remnant.

---

[1] See also Peters, W. R., *Mystical Medicine* and Steed, E. H. J., *Two Be One.* Both are available from Hartland Publications, Box 1, Rapidan, VA 22733.

4

Warnings of Spiritism in the Church

Shocking though it is, the servant of the Lord has given us many warnings against the inroads of Spiritism in our church. In ancient times, the children of Israel repeatedly returned to the spiritualistic practices of the pagans, and we are told that these practices will also come into the Seventh-day Adventist Church.

> At this crisis all are called upon to take their position. We must stand apart from those who are determined to make shipwreck of the faith. We must not sell our Lord at any price. We are to refuse to listen to the sophistries that have been brought in to make of no effect the truth for this time. Not a stone is to be moved in the foundation of the truth—not a pillar moved. . . . The time has come when even in the church and in our institutions, some will depart from the faith, giving heed to seducing spirits and doctrines of devils. But God will keep that which is committed to Him. . . . Through those who depart from the faith the power of the enemy will be exercised, to lead others astray
> (*Manuscript Releases*, vol. 7, p. 188).

It will be noted here, as in some subsequent statements, that to lead men and women away from the truth of God is referred to as Spiritism or the work of Spiritism. The shaking will commence with the introduction of false theories into the church (*Testimonies to Ministers*, p. 112). Little do most realize that this is fundamentally the work of the spiritualistic assault of Satan.

> Listen not a moment to the interpretations that would loosen one pin, remove one pillar, from the platform of truth. Human interpretation, the reception of fables, will spoil your faith, confuse your understanding, and make of none effect your faith in Jesus Christ. Study diligently the third chapter of Revelation. In it is pointed out the danger of losing your hold upon the things that you have heard and learned from the Source of all light (*Manuscript Releases*, vol. 1, p. 54–55).

When we were lads growing up, our parents warned us that every attack on the Adventist faith centered around the denial or perversion of the historic understanding of the ministry of Christ in the heavenly sanctuary. This has been a wonderful warning to us that has allowed us to see very quickly the direction of many of those who would bring false theories into the church.

> In the future, deception of every kind is to arise, and we want solid ground for our feet. We want solid pillars for the building. Not one pin is to be removed from that which the Lord has established. The enemy will bring in false theories, such as the doctrine that there is no sanctuary. This is one of the points on which there will be a departing from the faith. Where shall we find safety unless it be in the truths that the Lord has been giving for the last fifty years?
> *(Counsels to Writers and Editors, p. 53).*

Our church is now experiencing an emboldened attack upon the pillars of our faith, even by some men in high positions. Some are claiming that the sanctuary message and the Investigative Judgment are figments of the imagination of Sister White, that 1844 is a myth, that there is no actual sanctuary in heaven, and that Christ began the High Priestly ministry in A.D. 31. These amazing denials of Seventh-day Adventism all point to the fact that Spiritism has dramatically eroded the church. Not only does Spiritism come in through doctrine, but it also comes in via the methodologies and principles presented.

> And when men standing in the position of leaders and teachers work under the power of spiritualistic ideas and sophistries, shall we keep silent, for fear of injuring their influence, while souls are being beguiled? Satan will use every advantage that he can obtain to cause souls to become clouded and perplexed in regard to the work of the church, in regard to the word of God, in regard to the words of warning which He has given through the testimonies of His Spirit, to guard His little flock from the subtleties of the enemy
> *(Christian Leadership, p. 62).*

This statement asks some very central questions. Those who are speaking out today against the outrageous invasions of paganism into the Seventh-day Adventist Church are angrily declared to be critics and dividers of God's people. Many have cowered into silence because of such challenges. God asks, "Shall we keep silent for fear of injuring their influence, while souls are being beguiled?" To many, the upholding of false pastors and leaders is more important than the salvation of the flock that is being led into eternal destruction.

No matter how insignificant we may feel ourselves to be, no matter how ineffective may be our protest, God is calling us today to do what we can to warn our fellow church members against the beguiling influence of Satan in the church. If men claiming to be pastors, teachers, and ministers of the gospel are teaching "damnable heresies," there is a solemn obligation to meet them, oppose them, and warn the flock against them. High office does not give men the right to brandish their satanic sophistries before our people. It is a false concept of loyalty that is all too common that leads men and women to remain silent in such a time of spiritual crisis.

> Modern Spiritualism, resting upon the same foundation, is but a revival, in a new form, of the witchcraft and demon-worship that God condemned and prohibited of old. It is foretold in the Scriptures, which declare that "in the latter times some shall depart from the faith, giving heed to seducing spirits, and doctrines of devils." Paul, in his second letter to the Thessalonians, points to the special working of Satan in Spiritualism as an event to take place immediately before the second advent of Christ. Speaking of Christ's second coming, he declares that it is "after the working of Satan with all power and signs and lying wonders." And Peter, describing the dangers to which the church was to be exposed in the last days, says that as there were false prophets who led Israel into sin, so there will be false teachers, "who privily shall bring in damnable heresies, even denying the Lord that bought them. . . . And many shall follow their pernicious ways." Here the apostle has pointed out one of the marked characteristics of Spiritualist teachers (*Patriarchs and Prophets*, p. 686).

Note that those who bring in heresies are referred to by Sister White as "spiritualist teachers." Hardly any of us have understood how close is the introduction of the spurious philosophies and doctrines to the workings of spiritualistic agencies within our church.

> The line of distinction between professed Christians and the ungodly is now hardly distinguishable. Church members love what the world loves, and are ready to join with them; and Satan determines to unite them in one body, and thus strengthen his cause by sweeping all into the ranks of Spiritualism. Papists, who boast of miracles as a certain sign of the true church, will be readily deceived by this wonder-working power; and Protestants, having cast away the shield of truth, will also be deluded. Papists, Protestants, and worldlings will alike accept the form of godliness without the power, and they will see in this union a grand movement for the conversion of the world, and the ushering in of the long-expected millennium
> (*The Great Controversy,* pp. 588–589).

Do we think that Seventh-day Adventists will be immune to such deception? Are we already hurtling down the pathway of the papists and the apostate Protestants in accepting the form of godliness which is powerless to convert the soul and lead men and women to victory over satanic temptation? The insistence of myriads of ministers, teachers, and other leaders that we can sin until Jesus comes indicates the fact that Spiritism has all but taken over a major section of the Seventh-day Adventist Church.

Satanic delusions are embedding themselves in the minds of myriads of Seventh-day Adventists today. Those who have accepted as a fact that faithful and heaven-bound men and women will continue to sin until Jesus comes, have already accepted the great spiritualistic lie Satan first presented in the Garden of Eden. Many have been intimidated by warnings that belief in the power of Christ to keep His people from falling is legalism and perfectionism. However, the Bible leaves no doubt of God's power.

> Now unto him that is able to keep you from falling, and to present you faultless before the presence of his glory with exceeding joy (Jude 24).

> For the grace of God that bringeth salvation hath appeared to all men, teaching us that, denying ungodliness and worldly lusts, we should live soberly, righteously, and godly, in this present world (Titus 2:11–12).

> Who gave himself for us, that he might redeem us from all iniquity, and purify unto himself a peculiar people, zealous of good works (Titus 2:14).

> Husbands, love your wives, even as Christ also loved the church, and gave himself for it; that he might sanctify and cleanse it with the washing of water by the word, that he might present it to himself a glorious church, not having spot, or wrinkle, or any such thing; but that it should be holy and without blemish (Ephesians 5:25–27).
>
> Wherefore he is able also to save them to the uttermost that come unto God by him, seeing he ever liveth to make intercession for them (Hebrews 7:25).
>
> Whosoever is born of God doth not commit sin; for his seed remaineth in him: and he cannot sin, because he is born of God (1 John 3:9).

The sophistries of Satan continue to be thrust at the church. Here is a church that began under the message of Revelation 14:12.

> Here is the patience of the saints: here are they that keep the commandments of God, and the faith of Jesus (Revelation 14:12).

How can it be that such a people has been so twisted by wolves that have come in among the flock, that many have come to believe that it is impossible to keep the commandments? How can that text be twisted 180 degrees, to the thought that "here are they that *cannot* keep the commandments of God"? Only Satan could be responsible for such an evil teaching. When the glory of Christ and the angels fills the whole earth, these deceived ones, in terror, instead of crying "Lo, this is our God, we have waited for Him and He will save us," will be crying for the rocks and the mountains to fall upon them and hide them from the presence of the Lord. Their inexpressible anguish cannot be imagined. As these deceived ones recognize the deception of the false teachers, their fury against the unfaithful leaders will be unabated. The issue of keeping the commandments of God is the only way that we can correctly discriminate between the faithful and the unfaithful, between those who have been led by the Spirit of Christ and those who have been led by the spirit of Satan.

In talking to our colleges and schools, Sister White had this to say:

Satan is striving to gain every advantage. He desires to secure, not only students, but teachers. He has his plans laid. Disguised as an angel of light, he will walk the earth as a wonder-worker. In beautiful language he will present lofty sentiments. Good words will be spoken by him, and good deeds performed. Christ will be personified, but on one point there will be a marked distinction. Satan will turn the people from the law of God. Notwithstanding this, so well will he counterfeit righteousness, that if it were possible, he would deceive the very elect. Crowned heads, presidents, rulers in high places, will bow to his false theories. Instead of giving place to criticism, division, jealousy, and rivalry, those in our schools should be one in Christ. Only thus can they resist the temptations of the arch-deceiver
(*Fundamentals of Christian Education,* pp. 471–472).

Satan's assault is especially centered upon our schools. He realizes that our colleges and universities are the training grounds for the pastors, teachers, health workers, business leaders, and other workers in our church. He knows that if he can remove the light from the teachers, the students are going to be overwhelmingly deceived. In turn, as those students graduate and go out into the work of God, they will spread their spurious doctrines and attitudes among the flock of Christ. The difference between the methodology of Satan and the methodology of Christ is that Satan turns the people away from the law of God. That obviously means that men and women will be turned from keeping the law of God. Those who are proclaiming the sin-and-live theology are spiritualistic agents of Satan, attempting to destroy the very elect for whom Christ died. The very fact that rivalry and competition has become so pervasive in our schools, with the introduction of idolatrous sports programs and other such practices, indicates how far Spiritism has already permeated our educational system.

The whole philosophy of Christianity is inimical to such satanic influences in our educational system. What is taught and practiced in our colleges today is preached and taught in our pulpits tomorrow, and is believed and practiced by our people the day after tomorrow. Is it any wonder that these delusions of Satan have flooded with such unrestrained ease into the ranks of God's remnant church? The time has come for God's faithful people to arise and call men and women back to the old paths wherein is the good way (Jeremiah 6:16). Each member of the church of God who is awakened to the crisis hour in which we live must respond to this call.

5

Spiritism and the New Theology

The close links of Spiritism with the New Theology are rarely perceived by most Seventh-day Adventists. Many have failed to recognize that the sin-and-live theology is the most pervasive form of Spiritism in the world and the church. It was the sin-and-live theology that was presented to Adam and Eve in the Garden of Eden by Satan. Eve was told that if she disobeyed God by eating of the tree, she would not surely die, but would still live. Today, using all the cunning and sophistries accumulated in six thousand years of experimentation, Satan is presenting, in the most winning and persuasive way, the same concept that men and women can continue to sin until Jesus comes, and still be saved in the kingdom of heaven. As he makes his presentations, he is able to express the majority of his sophistries in truly dramatic ways through his servants. The final deception will be "confirmed" through his own impersonation of Christ. He will pretend loving and winning sentiments that only the very elect will resist.

Satan cannot bring himself to acknowledge the law of God. This law represents the very character of God. It is the transcript of that character. This is the character that Satan has maligned and has claimed is arbitrary and unloving. Therefore it is on this point alone that we can tell the difference between Satan's army and Christ's ambassadors. While the servants of Christ will point men and women to the sacred law of God and to the power of victory over sin that Christ provides through His death and ministry, the ambassadors of Satan will deny the saving power of Christ.

> The prophet Isaiah brings to view the fearful deception which will come upon the wicked, causing them to count themselves secure from the judgments of God: "We have made a covenant with death, and with hell are we at agreement; when the overflowing scourge shall pass through, it shall not come unto us: for we have made lies our refuge, and under falsehood have we hid ourselves." In the class here described are included those who in their stubborn impenitence comfort

themselves with the assurance that there is to be no punishment for the sinner; that all mankind, it matters not how corrupt, are to be exalted to heaven, to become as the angels of God. But still more emphatically are those making a covenant with death and an agreement with hell, who renounce the truths which Heaven has provided as a defense for the righteous in the day of trouble, and accept the refuge of lies offered by Satan in its stead—the delusive pretensions of Spiritualism (*The Great Controversy*, p. 560–561).

One has only to walk through the cemetery of any churchyard in the Christian world to realize the truth of this statement. It is almost impossible to find a tombstone which reads "Gone to hell." Most seem to have made their way to heaven. There are many such assurances as "At home with the Lord," "With Jesus," or "Resting in peace" engraved on many gravestones. It would seem that death brings instant sanctification, and that somehow, irrespective of how profligate the life may have been, the individual is instantaneously ready for the kingdom of heaven. However, such thinking is truly a covenant with death. The idea of Universalism, that all will be saved no matter what abominations they committed, is a fatal deception. The vast majority of supposed Christians will be shocked when, in the second resurrection, they recognize that that resurrection is not unto life but unto eternal destruction. While most Seventh-day Adventists do not espouse Universalism, nevertheless, a casual attitude to occasional sin will result in eternal loss by many expecting to be saved.

We believe that it is impossible for human beings to recognize the preparation that Satan has put into the deception of mankind. That satanic preparation is at least partially unveiled in the book, *The Great Controversy*.

Satan has long been preparing for his final effort to deceive the world. The foundation of his work was laid by the assurance given to Eve in Eden: "Ye shall not surely die." "In the day ye eat thereof, then your eyes shall be opened, and ye shall be as gods, knowing good and evil." Little by little he has prepared the way for his masterpiece of deception in the development of Spiritualism. He has not yet reached the full accomplishment of his designs; but it will be reached in the last remnant of time. Says the prophet: "I saw three unclean

> spirits like frogs; . . . they are the spirits of devils, working miracles, which go forth unto the kings of the earth and of the whole world, to gather them to the battle of that great day of God Almighty." Except those who are kept by the power of God, through faith in His word, the whole world will be swept into the ranks of this delusion. The people are fast being lulled into a fatal security, to be awakened only by the outpouring of the wrath of God
>
> (*The Great Controversy*, p. 561–562).

Satan has made an all-out effort to take control of the minds of people through the use of alcohol, mind-expanding and -destroying drugs, music, permissive sexual relations, and pornographic and sadistic literature. While some of these things are not used by most members of the church, many are trapped by television and the misuse of the computer. These are mesmerizing the minds of men and women, and driving them deeper and deeper into carnal security while they are moving headlong into eternal destruction.

We must not ignore the efforts of Satan to control every form of education. It is almost impossible today to carry on any course in a secular institution, and often in the institutions of the church, which is not undergirded by paganistic, spiritualistic, humanistic, New Age or evolutionary principles, all designed to deceive, and to derail the lives of unsuspecting human beings.

Spiritism reaches its greatest subtlety when Satan seeks to deceive those who are dedicated to Christ, who are members of the remnant.

> As Spiritualism more closely imitates the nominal Christianity of the day, it has greater power to deceive and ensnare. Satan himself is converted, after the modern order of things. He will appear in the character of an angel of light. Through the agency of Spiritualism, miracles will be wrought, the sick will be healed, and many undeniable wonders will be performed. And as the spirits will profess faith in the Bible, and manifest respect for the institutions of the church, their work will be accepted as a manifestation of divine power
>
> (*The Great Controversy*, p. 588).

The above statement was written especially for the fallen churches of Protestantism. As Seventh-day Adventism is drawn deeper and deeper into the ecumenical web, it faces the same dilemma, and the same consequences. People who have not fortified their minds with the Word of God, who have not taken the Bible, and the Bible only as their basis of practice, and who have listened to the sophistries of men rather than the pure word of truth, are drawn unsuspectingly into the deadly web of Satan.

No matter how subtle the attempt of Satan, no matter how perfectly he has laid his plans, there is no excuse for being deceived, no excuse for failing to stand firm, for the power of God is available to every human being without exception. The power of Christ is able to destroy every attempt of the evil one to undermine the confidence of our faith, and to lead us from the fold of Christ. We have been promised that He will not allow us to be taken out of His hand against our will (John 10:28). We know that He will never leave us nor forsake us (Hebrews 13:5), and therefore, with those assurances, and providing we never forsake Him, our victory is assured.

There has been no time in the history of the world when vigilance has been more necessary than in these last moments of probationary time. Our appeal is for every reader to daily consecrate himself to God and to the finishing of His work through witness to those who otherwise are moving in the pathway of death. The God of heaven patiently and longingly is waiting for His people to reflect His character so that Jesus might come to take us home to live with Him.

> When the character of Christ shall be perfectly reproduced in His people, then He will come to claim them as His own
> *(Christ's Object Lessons*, p. 69).

6

Adventists Begin to Waver on the State of the Dead

Satan has a very definite plan for derailing the principal doctrines of the Seventh-day Adventist Church. The plan is simple, but deadly in its effectiveness. Satan first begins by a time of quiescence. When we were lads growing up in the Seventh-day Adventist Church, we heard many sermons on the great pillars of the Adventist faith: on the Sabbath, the state of the dead, the commandments of God, the sanctuary, the Investigative Judgment, and the Second Coming. As the years have rolled by, however, less and less are these distinctives brought before our people. There are many who are brought into the church who do not know even the basics of such messages as the sanctuary and the Investigative Judgment. This condition is exacerbated by the fact that no longer do the baptismal vows more than casually address some of these issues, and, in some cases, they are ignored. There is little in the baptismal vows on the state of the dead. The Investigative Judgment is not even mentioned, neither do we have a statement on the power of Christ to provide victory over sin for every committed Christian. Thus, it is not unusual for men and women being prepared for baptism to be unaware of these great truths of the Seventh-day Adventist message, or at best to have a superficial knowledge of them.

Tragically, members' education in the message is often almost nil, if it is dependent upon the sermons being preached from the pulpit. The sanctuary message and the Investigative Judgment are almost never addressed in many pulpits today, and what the pastors do not emphasize as important, the laity is likely to ignore. This is especially true of those who have not had the grounding of earlier years.

The successful plan of Satan has been to allow a time of quiescence, a time of silence, when the distinctive messages are rarely proclaimed, and then to test the waters to see whether error can be introduced. It is obvious that when the flock are being well-fed and warned and indoctrinated by the powerful truths of the Scripture, they are not likely to be easy prey for the diabolical deceptions of Satan. However, if sufficient time has passed, and myriads of men and women have been brought into the church during that time with barely any knowledge of the truth, while others have become less and less concerned about the truths because they are not being given the primacy that God would that they have, then it is much easier to slowly, carefully, but determinedly bring the error into the church.

This has certainly happened in our understanding of the doctrine of the state of the dead. We ask the reader to consider how long it has been since he or she has heard a sermon on the state of the dead. Colin has asked this question in many parts of the world. He has asked it in many locations in the U.S.A., England, Norway, and around New Zealand and Australia, and in these locations there have often been representatives of twelve or more churches. The answer is that hardly anyone has heard such a sermon in the last twelve months, and most, not in the last five or ten years. Surely this period of silence on the state of the dead allows Satan to desensitize God's people to the great truth so that the final masterpiece of Satan's deception can be introduced. Surely this is a time when God's messengers, His pastors, His teachers, do well to prepare God's people for this insidious deception. Already the cracks are beginning to show in various parts of the world.

Colin was preaching in Indiana some years ago. After the sermon the pastor asked Colin to spend a little time with him. He then confided that his senior elder had only that week made the statement, "Pastor, there has to be more to death than just sleep." The pastor then asked Colin, "What do you think he meant?" Colin replied, "Pastor, you have got problems," to which the pastor responded, "That's what I think. What shall I do?" Colin suggested that he go back to the elder and say to him something like this: "I have been thinking about what you said to me last week concerning the state of the dead and, come to think of it, it has been a long time since I have preached a sermon on this theme. Maybe there are other people in the congregation who are uncertain about this topic too. So I have decided to preach three to five sermons on the topic to help the congregation understand what the Bible says on the state of the dead." With this approach the elder would recognize his pastor was trying to help him, not just trying to attack him. The pastor said that he would do this, and it is hoped that he did.

Clearly, this senior elder had significant influence in his church, and it is possible that he might already have been sharing his doubts with some of the members. Furthermore it was important for the pastor to open up such a topic for the congregation. Too often we take it for granted that our people know these doctrines well, and there is no need to go over old ground, but this assumption is false. Many only touched the periphery of some of the proof texts many years before when they were being prepared for baptism and they have not understood deeply the specific role of our belief on the state of the dead.

While preaching in Central California, Colin was approached by a number of people from one particular church. They said their Sabbath School teacher, a prominent professional in the Seventh-day Adventist Church and a member of the Conference Committee, had made the statement in the Sabbath School class, "We believe that when we die, we sleep awaiting the coming of the Lord. Some of my Pentecostal friends believe that we go straight to heaven when we die, but what does it matter? We all believe that ultimately we will be in the kingdom of heaven." That kind of statement shows the absolute lack of any understanding of the great significance of deception regarding the state of the dead to the final thrust of Satan to destroy the eternal hopes of humanity. Such a lack of discernment on the part of a prominent and respected layman shows how necessary it is for the pastors to spend significant amounts of time in their divine services as well as other studies in the prayer meeting that would alert all members to the end-time deceptions of Satan.

Recognizing that Spiritism will be the final deception, and that the Sabbath will be the final test of loyalty for God's people, these two themes should have an extraordinarily primary focus in the preaching of God's representatives.

In yet another sad experience, Russell was caring for a Chinese Thai businessman who had suffered several heart attacks. While Russell was president of the Bangkok Adventist Hospital, the man was re-admitted with a cardiac problem. One evening while his wife was visiting him, he suddenly had a major heart attack. The wife, in her desperation, demanded all the heroics possible, and Russell and the cardiac team did everything they could to resuscitate him. Though Russell believed that the efforts would be futile, to his great surprise, after about twenty-six minutes the man began to show some signs of reviving and indeed did revive into a dim twilight state. This was greatly appreciated by the wife, even though Russell explained to her that there was no chance of the husband surviving more than a very short period of time. However, it did give time for two sons, who were in the United States, to fly across and to be there when, sixteen days later, the man finally died.

During the period before his death, the youngest son, a graduate student at Loma Linda University, said to Russell, "I wonder where my dad was for those twenty-six minutes?" Russell was alarmed. He realized that this young man did not have a clear grip upon the message of the state of the dead. He discovered that the young man had been reading the spiritualistic writings of Elizabeth Kubler-Ross, and that he had accepted some concepts of after-death experiences. Russell spent at least half an hour explaining to him from the Bible the truth about the state of the dead. These examples serve to illustrate the fact that the security that Adventists once had on the state of the dead is not nearly as secure today.

One of Russell's colleagues returned home on furlough in 1991 and visited one of his children, who was attending a well-known Seventh-day Adventist College. He attended a Friday evening meeting where the doctrine of the state of the dead was raised to a panel of professors. The colleague heard no clear answer and was left with the impression that the professors believed that immediate life after death was as likely as a state of sleep.

Fewer and fewer messengers continue to explain, and to develop the understanding of congregations as to the true nature of man in death. And the cunning efforts of Satan at the end of time in presenting Spiritism, especially as he seeks to incorporate the children of light into the kingdom of darkness, will deceive more and more by his sophistries. It is essential that church members not rely upon their fellowmen, be they ministers or teachers, for a final understanding of these great truths.

Now is the time to study carefully the issues concerning the state of the dead. *The Great Controversy* brings Spiritism into clear focus in the chapters entitled, "Snares of Satan," "The Mystery of Immortality," "Can the Dead Speak to Us?"* These chapters need to be studied prayerfully and carefully to understand the sophistries of Satan and to keep us from his subtle deceptions.

---

* These are chapters 32–34 in the 1911 edition, and bear the titles "Snares of Satan," "The First Great Deception," and "Spiritualism."

7

The Bible Speaks

The Bible is unequivocal concerning man's state in death.* In clarion terms it presents the one certain fact that man is in an unconscious state, often referred to as sleep, during the time he waits between the end of his brief life upon this earth and the resurrection. The Bible denies the common concept that man has an immortal soul. Until the redemption of the saints, only God has immortality.

> Which in his times he shall shew, who is the blessed and only Potentate, the King of kings, and Lord of lords; who only hath immortality (1 Timothy 6:15–16).

The mortal state of fallen man is mentioned a number of times in the Bible.

> Shall mortal man be more just than God? (Job 4:17).

> Let not sin therefore reign in your mortal body (Romans 6:12).

> But if the Spirit of him that raised up Jesus from the dead dwell in you, he that raised up Christ from the dead shall also quicken your mortal bodies by his Spirit that dwelleth in you (Romans 8:11).

> For we which live are alway delivered unto death for Jesus' sake, that the life also of Jesus might be made manifest in our mortal flesh (2 Corinthians 4:11).

> For we that are in this tabernacle do groan, being burdened: not for that we would be unclothed, but clothed upon, that mortality might be swallowed up of life (2 Corinthians 5:4).

Once it is established that man is mortal, then it becomes clear that he does not have automatic eternal life; whether eternal life in heaven or in a fanciful, eternally burning hell. There are those who assume that these texts on mortality refer only to the body

---

* For a detailed study of this matter see R. R. and C. D. Standish, *The Mystery of Death*. Available from Hartland Publications, Box 1, Rapidan, VA 22733.

but not to the soul. But the Bible gives no mystical existence of the soul that is separate from the body. The Bible again clarifies that the soul is mortal.

> The soul that sinneth, it shall die (Ezekiel 18:4, 20).

Even the animals are referred to as having a soul.

> And every living soul died in the sea (Revelation 16:3).

In unmistakable terms God defines the word "soul."

> And the LORD God formed man of the dust of the ground, and breathed into his nostrils the breath of life; and man became a living soul (Genesis 2:7).

It was this issue of mortality that became the centerpiece of the deception of Satan. God had explained to Adam that if he disobeyed by eating from the tree of the knowledge of good and evil, he would die.

> And the LORD God commanded the man, saying, Of every tree of the garden thou mayest freely eat: but of the tree of the knowledge of good and evil, thou shalt not eat of it: for in the day that thou eatest thereof thou shalt surely die (Genesis 2:16–17).

And it was this warning of God that Satan challenged when through the serpent he asked the question:

> Yea, hath God said, Ye shall not eat of every tree of the garden? (Genesis 3:1).

Eve actually went beyond the statement of God when she said,

> We may eat of the fruit of the trees of the garden: but of the fruit of the tree which is in the midst of the garden, God hath said, Ye shall not eat of it, neither shall ye touch it, lest ye die (Genesis 3:2–3).

Then for the first time on this planet Satan presented his direct contradiction of God in a lie that he has repeated down through the six thousand years of history:

> Ye shall not surely die: for God doth know that in the day ye eat thereof, then your eyes shall be opened, and ye shall be as gods, knowing good and evil (Genesis 3:4–5).

Tragically, Eve accepted the word of the arch-deceiver against the immutable word of God. And with prodigal credulity the majority of the human race has continued to accept Satan's lie. It was this lie that led to the fall of the human race and to death. And it is the same lie that will lead to eternal death. Paul emphasizes that,

> The wages of sin is death (Romans 6:23).

> Wherefore, as by one man sin entered into the world, and death by sin; and so death passed upon all men, for that all have sinned (Romans 5:12).

While all wicked and righteous alike die this first death, only the wicked die the eternal death of oblivion at the final judgment of God.

> Who shall be punished with everlasting destruction from the presence of the Lord, and from the glory of his power
> (2 Thessalonians 1:9).

Whereas God is the ruler of life, Satan is the ruler over death. For he is the one that is responsible for it.

> Forasmuch then as the children are partakers of flesh and blood, he also himself likewise took part of the same; that through death he might destroy him that had the power of death, that is, the devil (Hebrews 2:14).

In many texts of scripture the condition of the dead is defined.

> For the living know that they shall die: but the dead know not any thing, neither have they any more a reward; for the memory of them is forgotten. Also their love, and their hatred, and their envy, is now perished; neither have they any more a portion for ever in any thing that is done under the sun
> (Ecclesiastes 9:5–6).

> So man lieth down, and riseth not: till the heavens be no more, they shall not awake, nor be raised out of their sleep
> (Job 14:12).

> His sons come to honour, and he knoweth it not; and they are brought low, but he perceiveth it not of them (Job 14:21).

> His breath goeth forth, he returneth to his earth; in that very day his thoughts perish (Psalm 146:4).

> For in death there is no remembrance of thee: in the grave who shall give thee thanks? (Psalm 6:5).
>
> The dead praise not the LORD, neither any that go down into silence (Psalm 115:17).

In the Bible many times death is referred to as sleep, the state of unconsciousness where man is unaware of the events that occur after he dies.

> And many of them that sleep in the dust of the earth shall awake, some to everlasting life, and some to shame and everlasting contempt (Daniel 12:2).
>
> He saith unto them, Our friend Lazarus sleepeth; but I go, that I may awake him out of sleep. Then said his disciples, Lord, if he sleep, he shall do well. Howbeit Jesus spake of his death: but they thought that he had spoken of taking of rest in sleep. Then said Jesus unto them plainly, Lazarus is dead (John 11:11-14).
>
> But I would not have you to be ignorant, brethren, concerning them which are asleep, that ye sorrow not, even as others which have no hope (1 Thessalonians 4:13).

Some have turned to obscure texts in an attempt to sustain the concept of immediate life after death. But never should the unclear texts be used to contradict the clear testimonies of such a wide range of biblical evidence.

Commonly used is the parable of the rich man and Lazarus in Luke 16:20-31. But even a quick reading of this parable clarifies the fact that it is not describing an actual situation, but rather some fable of the day. Such language as,

> And was carried by the angels into Abraham's bosom (Luke 16:22),

evidences the fact that this is not a real experience. Further, verse 24 indicates the likelihood that Lazarus could somehow be close enough to place water on the tongue of the dead man. It is the principle that Christ is explaining in this parable that is important. The parable deals with the principle that what we do in this life determines our eternal destiny. It will be too late, after we have died to change the characters that we have formed during the years of our earthly life.

Some have claimed that the Bible teaches an eternally burning hell. For example,

> And the smoke of their torment ascendeth up for ever and ever: and they have no rest day nor night, who worship the beast and his image, and whosoever receiveth the mark of his name (Revelation 14:11).

But it should be recognized that this concept of ever and ever means only until the total disposition of the situation. Putting it another way, the consequences and results are everlasting. This can be well understood with the following text.

> Even as Sodom and Gomorrha, and the cities about them in like manner, giving themselves over to fornication, and going after strange flesh, are set forth for an example, suffering the vengeance of eternal fire (Jude 7).

While this text says that Sodom and Gomorrha suffered the vengeance of eternal fire, in reality the fires did not burn eternally; but the consequences of those fires are eternal. The cities of Sodom and Gomorrha will never be rebuilt. They have been destroyed forever.

In the clearest terms we are told by Paul that those who die are destroyed eternally.

> Who shall be punished with everlasting destruction from the presence of the Lord, and from the glory of his power (2 Thessalonians 1:9).

It will be noted that not only is the destruction everlasting, but it is destruction "from," not "in" the presence of the Lord.

One cannot deny that the text often used by Mormons to validate their members being baptized for others who have lived before, a practice which has led the Mormons into deep research of genealogies, is on the surface a difficult text.

> Else what shall they do which are baptized for the dead, if the dead rise not at all? why are they then baptized for the dead? (1 Corinthians 15:29).

What makes this text difficult is that it is the only time in the Bible that there is even the slightest reference to Paul's subject here. That makes it difficult for us to understand the full impact of what Paul is trying to say. Almost certainly he is responding to a specific situation that was well understood by the Corinthians, but which we do not understand today.

It would not be unreasonable to place this question in the context of verse 31:

> I die daily (1 Corinthians 15:31).

Yet even this text cannot explain what Paul was saying here. But it is certain that no one can be baptized for someone else's salvation, for there would be no change in the character or the eternal destiny of someone who was dead because of the baptism of a living person. Many explanations have been attempted on this text but it may well be that we will have to wait until the kingdom to get the clear understanding of what Paul was saying. But in the light of the overwhelming, clear and unequivocal texts on the state of the dead, this text cannot be allowed to be a stumbling block to anyone who seriously wants to follow the truth of God on this topic.

Such texts are only used by Satan to mislead so that his deadly error of human immortality can be used to entrap men and women for eternal destruction.

8

The Resurrection and Immortality

Throughout the Bible, the concept of eternal life and immortality is riveted upon the sacrificial ministry of Jesus Christ.

> For God so loved the world, that he gave his only begotten Son, that whosoever believeth in him should not perish, but have everlasting life (John 3:16).

> For the wages of sin is death; but the gift of God is eternal life through Jesus Christ our Lord (Romans 6:23).

To the faithful are the wonderful promises of an eternal life with the One who died for us.

> Let not your heart be troubled: ye believe in God, believe also in me. In my Father's house are many mansions: if it were not so, I would have told you. I go to prepare a place for you. And if I go and prepare a place for you, I will come again, and receive you unto myself; that where I am, there ye may be also (John 14:1–3).

The One who created us, giving us life, is the One who will bring to us eternal life.

> Seeing he giveth to all life, and breath, and all things (Acts 17:25).

> But is now made manifest by the appearing of our Saviour Jesus Christ, who hath abolished death, and hath brought life and immortality to light through the gospel (2 Timothy 1:10).

Jesus Himself made these issues very real to His hearers.

> Verily, verily, I say unto you, The hour is coming, and now is, when the dead shall hear the voice of the Son of God: and they that hear shall live. For as the Father hath life in himself; so hath he given to the Son to have life in himself; and hath given him authority to execute judgment also, because he is the Son of man. Marvel not at this: for the hour is coming, in the which all that are in the graves shall hear his

> voice, and shall come forth; they that have done good, unto
> the resurrection of life; and they that have done evil, unto the
> resurrection of damnation (John 5:25–29).

The Bible, while normally referring to just two resurrections, actually details three. There is to be a little resurrection immediately prior to the coming of Jesus. In this resurrection, those who were specifically responsible for the crucifixion of Jesus will be alive to see Him coming in power and great glory.

> Behold, he cometh with clouds; and every eye shall see him,
> and they also which pierced him: and all kindreds of the earth
> shall wail because of him (Revelation 1:7).

And too we have the assurance that those who have died in the hope of the three angels' messages will be resurrected just prior to the coming of the Lord in this special resurrection.

> Graves are opened, and "many of them that sleep in the dust
> of the earth . . . awake, some to everlasting life, and some to
> shame and everlasting contempt." All who have died in the
> faith of the third angel's message come forth from the tomb
> glorified, to hear God's covenant of peace with those who
> have kept His law (*The Great Controversy*, p. 637).

However, there are two major resurrections. They are spoken of by the prophet Daniel.

> And many of them that sleep in the dust of the earth shall
> awake, some to everlasting life, and some to shame and everlasting contempt (Daniel 12:2).

This is also spoken of by Paul.

> And have hope toward God, which they themselves also allow, that there shall be a resurrection of the dead, both of the
> just and unjust (Acts 24:15).

> Marvel not at this: for the hour is coming, in the which all
> that are in the graves shall hear his voice, and shall come
> forth; they that have done good, unto the resurrection of life;
> and they that have done evil, unto the resurrection of damnation (John 5:28–29).

For those who have been faithful and loyal to God, the resurrection brings eternal life.

The Resurrection and Immortality

> For the wages of sin is death; but the gift of God is eternal life through Jesus Christ our Lord (Romans 6:23).

Those who will receive the gift of eternal life are those whose names are written in the book of life. But the destiny is tragically different for those whose names are not in the book of life.

> And whosoever was not found written in the book of life was cast into the lake of fire (Revelation 20:15).

Just as there are two groups of people, there are two resurrections. The righteous who will be saved eternally are resurrected in the first resurrection.

> And they lived and reigned with Christ a thousand years (Revelation 20:4).

But the wicked are resurrected a thousand years later.

> But the rest of the dead lived not again until the thousand years were finished. This is the first resurrection. Blessed and holy is he that hath part in the first resurrection: on such the second death hath no power, but they shall be priests of God and of Christ, and shall reign with him a thousand years (Revelation 20:5–6).

During that thousand-year period the righteous will be reviewing the records of fallen men and fallen angels.

> And I saw thrones, and they [the saints] sat upon them, and judgment was given unto them (Revelation 20:4).

Paul also understood this judgment when he said,

> Do ye not know that the saints shall judge the world? (1 Corinthians 6:2).

> Know ye not that we shall judge angels? (1 Corinthians 6:3).

The judgment that takes place through the thousand years is a judgment in which the saints have the opportunity to review the records. Daniel testifies that the unfallen beings of the universe prior to the salvation of the saints, have had the opportunity to review the heavenly records.

> I beheld till the thrones were cast down, and the Ancient of days did sit, whose garment was white as snow, and the hair of his head like the pure wool: his throne was like the fiery flame, and his wheels as burning fire. A fiery stream issued and came forth from before him: thousand thousands ministered unto him, and ten thousand times ten thousand [of angels, see Revelation 5:11] stood before him: the judgment was set, and the books were opened (Daniel 7:9-10).

Here we can see that the angels had the opportunity to review the records in the judgment of God. God does not save one soul for eternity before the angels have been convinced that God's justice has been perfect; that those who are saved are safe to save, and that those who are lost had every opportunity, which they neglected or rejected, for their eternal salvation. But now the saints, during the thousand years, will be in heaven in the mansions that God has prepared for them and they will have the opportunity to review the records of fallen men and angels. It is not that God has made any mistakes; but God in His infinite wisdom is securing eternity so that there will never be the slightest doubt that everything was done that could be done for the salvation of men and women.

After this comes the second resurrection. The wicked, under the leadership of the fallen angel, Lucifer, try to destroy the saints who have come down with Christ out of heaven in the New Jerusalem.

> And they went up on the breadth of the earth, and compassed the camp of the saints about, and the beloved city: and fire came down from God out of heaven, and devoured them (Revelation 20:9).

But what a difference it is for the saints. Hear these wonderful passages of Scripture.

> But now is Christ risen from the dead, and become the firstfruits of them that slept. For since by man came death, by man came also the resurrection of the dead. For as in Adam all die, even so in Christ shall all be made alive. But every man in his own order: Christ the firstfruits; afterward they that are Christ's at his coming (1 Corinthians 15:20-23).

The Resurrection and Immortality

> Behold, I shew you a mystery; We shall not all sleep, but we shall all be changed, in a moment, in the twinkling of an eye, at the last trump: for the trumpet shall sound, and the dead shall be raised incorruptible, and we shall be changed. For this corruptible must put on incorruption, and this mortal must put on immortality. So when this corruptible shall have put on incorruption, and this mortal shall have put on immortality, then shall be brought to pass the saying that is written, Death is swallowed up in victory (1 Corinthians 15:51–54).

This is the eternal life of which Christ spoke.

> But they which shall be accounted worthy to obtain that world, and the resurrection from the dead, neither marry, nor are given in marriage: neither can they die any more: for they are equal unto the angels; and are the children of God, being the children of the resurrection (Luke 20:35–36).

To the apostles, the all-consuming hope was the resurrection. Paul stated,

> For the Lord himself shall descend from heaven with a shout, with the voice of the archangel, and with the trump of God: and the dead in Christ shall rise first: then we which are alive and remain shall be caught up together with them in the clouds, to meet the Lord in the air: and so shall we ever be with the Lord (1 Thessalonians 4:16–17).

James expressed this truth as follows:

> Be patient therefore, brethren, unto the coming of the Lord. Behold, the husbandman waiteth for the precious fruit of the earth, and hath long patience for it, until he receive the early and latter rain. Be ye also patient; stablish your hearts: for the coming of the lord draweth nigh (James 5:7–8).

Peter likewise longed for the coming of the Lord.

> Seeing then that all these things shall be dissolved, what manner of persons ought ye to be in all holy conversation and godliness, looking for and hasting unto the coming of the day of God, wherein the heavens being on fire shall be dissolved, and the elements shall melt with fervent heat? Nevertheless we, according to his promise, look for new heavens and a new

> earth, wherein dwelleth righteousness. Wherefore, beloved, seeing that ye look for such things, be diligent that ye may be found of him in peace, without spot, and blameless
>
> (2 Peter 3:11–14).

John's longing was expressed succinctly.

> He which testifieth these things saith, Surely I come quickly. Amen. Even so, come, Lord Jesus (Revelation 22:20).

Jude added the following:

> But ye, beloved, building up yourselves on your most holy faith, praying in the Holy Ghost, keep yourselves in the love of God, looking for the mercy of our Lord Jesus Christ unto eternal life (Jude 20–21).

If there were immediate life after death, the issue of the Second Coming would take upon itself little significance. But the Second Coming is the hope, the blessed hope, as Paul called it in Titus 2:13, the consummation of every earnest petition of all Christ's faithful people, the reason for His death and for His ministry in behalf of each one of us. The concept of immediate life after death falls into disrepute, since the writers of the New Testament concentrate upon the centrality of the return of Jesus Christ and the glorious blessing that God has for each one of us. The concept of immediate life after death cannot stand against the united focus of the apostles upon Christ's second coming. It is our beautiful opportunity to prepare our own lives that we might honor God and show our thankfulness by being ready to live with Jesus throughout eternity.

9

The Development of Spiritism in the Christian Church

From his first success in the introduction of Spiritism in the Garden of Eden, Satan has never wavered in his continual effort to destroy the confidence of man in the Word of God and to place his spiritualistic principles into the minds of men who have not allowed Christ to become the Lord of their lives. The descendants of Cain followed the principles of Satan, and, for many years, his descendants remained separate from the descendants of Seth.

> But in the lapse of time they ventured, little by little, to mingle with the inhabitants of the valleys. This association was productive of the worst results. "The sons of God saw the daughters of men that they were fair." The children of Seth, attracted by the beauty of the daughters of Cain's descendants, displeased the Lord by intermarrying with them. Many of the worshipers of God were beguiled into sin by the allurements that were now constantly before them, and they lost their peculiar, holy character. Mingling with the depraved, they became like them in spirit and in deeds; the restrictions of the seventh commandment were disregarded, "and they took them wives of all which they chose" (*Patriarchs and Prophets,* p. 81).

But step by step the church of the antediluvian world became contaminated and corrupted by the evil of the worldlings until their distinction was virtually unnoticeable. Pagan practices became commonplace and Satan soon had control of the overwhelming majority of earth's inhabitants.

After the earth was cleansed by the flood, only eight human beings remained. But it is alarming to note the rapidity with which Satan was able to reintroduce the elements of paganism, and with it the degrading aspects of Spiritism into the human race. None was more responsible for this than Nimrod. Nimrod is little mentioned in the Scripture. The Bible says Nimrod was a mighty hunter (Genesis 10:9), but his greatest accomplishments were to build four cities near what is now the Persian Gulf—Babylon, Erech, Accad, Calneh (Genesis 10:10).

More than anyone else in the post-diluvian world, Nimrod, known in history as Ninus or Nimrud, was the perpetrator of paganism and Spiritism in the world. In establishing what became the Babylonian and Assyrian civilizations, he laid the foundation of the paganism and Spiritism which is engulfing the modern world today. The gods of Babylon were reproduced by the Phoenicians, the Egyptians, the Greeks, and the Romans. Through Rome paganism invaded the Christian church, becoming imbedded in Roman Catholicism and much of it passing into Protestantism of a later time. There has frequently been a fascination by some of the people of God with such Spiritism.

In spite of the warnings of God through Moses, spiritualistic practices were soon found invading the Children of Israel. The marriage of many of the Israelites with pagans was soon to affect the purity of the Israelite people. After the division of the kingdom there was never again a king in Israel who did not lead the people into this spiritualistic worship. In Judah there were some faithful kings, but nevertheless, from time to time paganistic Spiritism was to have strong reign in the nation through the practices of their apostate kings.

After the restoration following the Babylonian captivity, every effort was made to keep paganistic practices out of Israel, and yet spirit possession was not uncommon at the time of Christ. During the ministry of the apostles they faced witchcraft and pagan practices commonly. By the grace of God many were drawn from these evil practices.

The writers of the New Testament did everything they could to establish the truth on the state of the dead, and to assure their hearers and readers that the whole hope of the Christian pivoted upon the return of Jesus. Very vivid was the hope of the Second Coming which many expected would occur in the days of the apostles. Indeed, a statement from Jesus to the disciples had convinced many that the apostle John would be alive at the return of Jesus. John had to deny this.

> Then Peter, turning about, seeth the disciple whom Jesus loved following; which also leaned on his breast at supper, and said, Lord, which is he that betrayeth thee? Peter seeing him saith to Jesus, Lord, and what shall this man do? Jesus saith unto him, If I will that he tarry till I come, what is that to thee?

follow thou me. Then went this saying abroad among the brethren, that that disciple should not die: yet Jesus said not unto him, He shall not die; but, If I will that he tarry till I come, what is that to thee? (John 21:20–23).

It is not difficult to imagine the great distress that swept across the Christians of early times when word eventually reached them that the last of the apostles, John, had died and Jesus had not returned. As the days moved into weeks, the weeks into months, the months into years, the years into decades, the decades into centuries, less and less were men and women buoyed by hope of the return of Jesus. More and more the Second Coming of Jesus as the central theme of the Christian message, was lost. Teachers arose who gave scant attention to this topic and spent their time dissecting and analyzing beyond reason the meaning the Word of God, often bringing out concepts that were contrary to the true meaning of the Words of Inspiration.

As so little was said about the Second Coming of Christ, it was not difficult for Satan to infuse, step by step the pagan concept of immediate life after death. Soon the great truths of the Bible were lost as men and women eagerly accepted the concept that immediately upon death they would be translated to heaven. The concept of immortality and the immortal soul became fixed in the minds of men and women and they cherished the thought that the soul would never die and would go immediately to heaven upon death. There was a brief renewal of interest in the return of Jesus at the turn of the first millennium of the Christian era as men wondered if that would be the time for the return of Jesus, but such a hope soon vanished away.

With the advent of the Reformation, as men and women placed their focus upon the study of the Bible, many discovered the falsity of the papal claim of immediate life after death. Thus today, scattered throughout Europe, are many gravestones which attest to the fact that there was a resurgence of the belief that death is a sleep with the departed one waiting for the return of Jesus to be renewed to life again. Colin on one occasion while visiting England saw on a seventeenth century gravestone the words "He sleepeth until Jesus comes."

But as the years, decades and centuries rolled by, Protestantism soon returned to the pagan concept of immediate life after death. With the rise of the Seventh-day Adventist Church and its emphasis upon the Bible, and the Bible only as its basis of faith and practice, there was renewed recognition of the true nature of man in death. God raised up a people who would have a message to defy the final temptations of Satan and to warn people against the cunning deceptiveness of spiritism. This precious message must be held inviolate by everyone who will be ready to meet Jesus. It is a message that not only must be proclaimed frequently, but must be shared with the inhabitants of the world. It is only to be expected, however, that Satan will do everything he can to undermine the confidence in the truth of the state of the dead among Seventh-day Adventists. It is our responsibility to teach it with great conviction so that men and women will not be deceived.

10

Minds Will Be Hypnotized

No greater effort will be exerted by Satan in the last times than in the area of hypnotism. It is the most effective method of drawing men and women under his control and power. It is well known that some people are far more suggestible than others and therefore much more vulnerable to hypnotic suggestion. It may well be that there are some so resistant to suggestion that no human being could hypnotize them. However, we must recognize that the master hypnotist, Satan, is able to hypnotize every single human being. There is only one way that we can have certainty that we will not be deceived by Satan, and that is by inviting Christ to take full control of our lives. Thus the Scripture says,

> Let this mind be in you, which was also in Christ Jesus
> (Philippians 2:5).

The mind of Christ could never be hypnotized by Satan, and therefore could not be deceived. If we invite Christ's mind to be our mind, then that alone will preserve us from the hypnotic presentations of Satan. The servant of the Lord warned us,

> The experience of the past will be repeated. In the future Satan's superstitions will assume new forms. Errors will be presented in a pleasing and flattering manner. False theories, clothed with garments of light, will be presented to God's people. Thus Satan will try to deceive, if possible, the very elect. Most seducing influences will be exerted; minds will be hypnotized   (*Maranatha*, p. 59).

This passage is not talking about the world at large; it is talking about members of the Seventh-day Adventist Church. It is fair to deduce that every individual on the face of this planet will be hypnotized by Satan with one group excluded—those whose names are written in the book of life.

In Satan's last great effort, all are going to be deceived by his hypnotic influence and the influence of his representatives. Thus, there will be an apparent unison that will bring the world together to worship the Papacy, referred to as the beast power in Revelation 13.

> And all that dwell upon the earth shall worship him, whose names are not written in the book of life of the Lamb slain from the foundation of the world (Revelation 13:8).

Surely only mass hypnotism could lead the inhabitants of this world into one bond of worship. This brings together the Atheists and the Agnostics, the Animists, the Muslims, the Shintoists, the Taoists, the Buddhists, the Hindus, the Zoroastrians, the Protestants, the Catholics, and every non-committed person in the world. This will be the greatest mass-hypnotism of all ages. Sadly, myriads of those who once walked in the light of the Advent faith, but who have not surrendered their lives to Christ, will also be hypnotized at this point.

Almost ninety years ago Sister White sensed the great inroads of hypnotism in the Adventist Church.

> This same hypnotic influence is seen working among our people today. Ever since my return to America a heavy burden has rested upon me. Everywhere I see the power of the enemy. Were it not for the armies of the Lord's host, led by Michael, the destruction that Satan would be pleased to witness would come to the people of God. They would be discomfited and brought to shame. But the Lord will work for His people. He will not suffer them to be defeated
> (*Manuscript Releases*, vol. 11, p. 248).

As the decades have passed, the intensification of Satan's efforts to hypnotize have unquestionably led to more and more Adventists coming under his hypnotic spell. As men and women move more and more to the world, and less and less place their confidence in Christ, there are deep inroads of Spiritism in the church through the power of hypnosis.

As early as 1870 Sister White referred to the efforts of Satan to hypnotize God's people. She remarked,

> Some seem to have no power to keep their eyes open in meeting. Satan seems to mesmerize them when important truths are presented (*Review and Herald,* March 29, 1870).

Thus the inroad of Spiritism into our church is not new.
Again during the first decade of this century Sister White refers to the hypnotic influence exerted by Dr. Kellogg.

> The men who sustain Dr. Kellogg are in a half-mesmerized condition, and do not understand the condition of the man. They honestly believe that he is to be trusted (Arthur White, *The Later Elmshaven Years 1905-1915*, vol. 6, p. 72).

You may have wondered why it is that you can present the clearest, most unambiguous statement of the Bible or the Spirit of Prophecy to men and women, and somehow they do not seem to be able to understand its meaning or its significance, or they are able to rationalize it away. Surely already so many have been hypnotized by Satan that they cannot perceive the certainty of God's truth.

> Satan is waiting to steal a march upon everyone who allows himself to be deceived by his hypnotism. He begins to exert his power over them just as soon as they begin to investigate his theories (*Medical Ministry,* pp. 101–102).

This statement indicates the danger of even exploring areas of error and apostasy. Satan is there to try to draw us into his trap by the use of hypnotism.

Colin remembers three of his former friends or colleagues, all of whom decided that they would help people who had moved away from the truth and who had accepted the evangelical concepts of the New Theology. All three of them have joined the ranks of these evangelicals. Rather than helping the one who was deceived, they were themselves equally deceived. It is a wholly unsafe practice to dabble in the artifices of Satan. One has an obligation personally to investigate; but once error is detected, it is unsafe to continue such a study.

Predicting what would take place right at the end of time the servant of the Lord said,

> This entering in of Satan through the sciences is well devised. Through the channel of phrenology, psychology, and mesmerism, he comes more directly to the people of this genera-

tion, and works with that power which is to characterize his efforts near the close of probation. The minds of thousands have thus been poisoned, and led into infidelity

(Selected Messages, Book 2, p. 351).

How important it is that we do not allow our minds to come under the control of others, for in so doing we are coming under the power of Satan.

> Satan often finds a powerful agency for evil in the power which one human mind is capable of exerting on another human mind. This influence is so seductive that the person who is being molded by it is often unconscious of its power. God has bidden me speak warning against this evil, that His servants may not come under the deceptive power of Satan. The enemy is a master worker, and if God's people are not constantly led by the Spirit of God, they will be snared and taken.
>
> For thousands of years Satan has been experimenting upon the properties of the human mind, and he has learned to know it well. By his subtle workings in these last days, he is linking the human mind with his own, imbuing it with his thoughts; and he is doing this work in so deceptive a manner that those who accept his guidance know not that they are being led by him at his will. The great deceiver hopes so to confuse the minds of men and women, that none but his voice will be heard *(Selected Messages,* Book 2, pp. 352–353).

On a number of occasions Ellen White wrote testimonies to physicians who were using hypnosis and other mind control techniques. She indicated the danger of these, and yet today there are some of our Seventh-day Adventist doctors who are routinely exercising an hypnotic influence over their patients all in the name of medicine.

In *Medical Ministry* she wrote as follows,

> Now, my brother, I consider you to be in positive peril. I present this because I know that you are in great danger of being seduced by Satan. We are living in a time when every phase of fanaticism will press its way in among believers and unbelievers. Satan will come in, speaking lies in hypocrisy. Everything that he can invent to deceive men and women will be brought forward.

> Just in proportion as men lose their sense of the need of vital religion, so they become filled with common, earthly ideas, which they exalt as wonderful knowledge. Physicians who lose their hold on Christ become filled with ideas of their own, which they look upon as some wonderful science to be brought into the medical profession as something new and strange (*Medical Ministry*, p. 114).

Some Seventh-day Adventists have thought nothing about going to a hypnotist to seek help in psychological problems, and even for various forms of child and marriage counseling. But such is the work of Satan. We are to have nothing to do with these practices.

Colin recalls talking on the telephone in 1974 to John Roth, whose life was almost destroyed by his attendance at a mind-control program. Mr. Roth was at the time, an orthodox Jew and in middle-management in an oil company. Wanting to improve his status in life, he accepted the recommendation of a friend to attend a Silva mind-control program. Having paid several hundred dollars for the program, he eagerly attended. The first night a very well-presented man stood before them and explained that we only use approximately six percent of all the neurons we have during our lifetime and that this program was to help to expand dramatically the use of the neurons in our brain.

It all sounded very good and Mr. Roth couldn't wait until the second day. On the second day all those who were in attendance were asked to imagine that they had a counselor and to decide what kind of questions they would like to ask such a counselor. By the third night the instructor was not talking about an imagined counselor, he was talking about "your counselor."

Being an Orthodox Jew, Mr. Roth was rather disturbed by this and called his friend who invited him over to his place and told him that this was the best part of the program; that he got such wonderful advice from his counselor. He then asked Mr. Roth, "What question would you like me to ask my counselor?" Mr. Roth almost off-handedly said, "Ask your counselor what I will be doing in twelve months time." He watched his friend go into a trance-like state, no doubt built upon auto-hypnosis. After a while he was deeply concerned by the obvious agitation of his friend, and wondered what was taking place. Shortly afterward his friend came out of the trance-like state and said, "I don't know what happened. My counselor has been so kind and so helpful to me, but when I asked your question all he did was curse and swear." This did not encourage Mr. Roth, but having paid so much money for the course he attended the fourth and fifth nights. Before the program was over they had been led into levitation and astral projection (out-of-body experiences).

Almost immediately Mr. Roth became ill; in fact, so ill that he had to be admitted to the hospital. But there the doctors could find no physical problem. And yet, clearly, his vital forces were diminishing and they had to concede that he was dying. This, you can understand, brought great worry to himself and to his wife. One night they were visited by Christian friends. The friends were shocked to see the state of Mr. Roth and as they talked with the wife, she told them what had taken place and that they had associated this sickness with the program that he had attended. The Christian friends said, "There is one answer to this, but you may not like it, and that is to pray in the name of Jesus."

Eventually she agreed and they went back to the bedside of Mr. Roth and asked if he would agree, which he did. So that night they prayed in the name of Christ that he would be released from the Satanic power that was destroying his life. Virtually immediately he began to recover. The physicians could give no explanation for his recovery any more than they could of his original illness. The Roths accepted Christianity and Mr. Roth became a major speaker around the United States telling people of his salvation from the satanic influence over his life.

No doubt, some way, somehow, the spirit that was the counselor of his friend, who had cursed and sworn when asked what Mr. Roth would be doing in twelve months time realized what would take place.

In his book, *The Seduction of Christianity,* David Hunt quotes one of the world's leading occult authorities and historians, Manly P. Hall, who declared,

> There is abundant evidence that in many forms of modern thought—especially the so-called "prosperity psychology" "will-power building" metaphysics and systems of "high-pressure"

salesmanship—black magic has merely passed through a metamorphosis, and although its name may be changed, its nature remains the same (David Hunt, *The Seduction of Christianity*, p. 14).

More and more Seventh-day Adventists seek worldly help for their spiritual problems, which often are designated emotional problems. In reality these stress and emotional issues are the symptoms of a lack of spiritual depth in the life. What men and women need much more than human counselors and psychologists is the power of the indwelling Christ in the life.

Colin well knows the simple means that Satan uses to hypnotize people. As an undergraduate student of the University of Sydney, he studied a little into the areas of suggestion and hypnosis. One night, in a group of Adventist youth, he was asked if he could hypnotize. Foolishly, he responded, "Of course," never thinking that anything would take place. As he chose one of the young ladies and used the very simplest of techniques that had been explained in class, he was terrified by the fact that she soon entered a deep hypnotic state. Also, the young people watching from the darkness outside the window were terrified when they saw what took place. They came rushing into the room, urging Colin to bring the young lady out of that hypnotic state. Colin was uncertain of what to do, but in the end, given the command to wake up, she did wake up. He had to ask the forgiveness of the Lord and to make a commitment never to allow such a thing to happen again.

Most people unfamiliar with hypnosis believe it is an extraordinarily difficult art. But in reality it is simple and commonly used today in all sorts of aspects of life, including advertising, interpersonal relations, and counseling.

If ever there was a time when God's people need the mind of Christ, it is now. Hypnotism is surely the strongest avenue to lead men and women to be deceived by Spiritism. Indeed, the two are indivisibly linked one with the other. God's people are called to keep clear of any form of hypnotism, mind control or human methods of handling the problems and issues of life.

11

Spiritism and Devil Possession

Through the history of the Scriptures, especially in the time of Christ and the apostles, there are many cases presented of devil possession. In Christ's day, for example, devil possession was manifested through dumbness.

> As they went out, behold, they brought to him a dumb man possessed with a devil (Matthew 9:32).

Another time the devil possession gave the evidence of insanity.

> And when he was come to the other side into the country of the Gergesenes, there met him two possessed with devils, coming out of the tombs, exceeding fierce, so that no man might pass by that way (Matthew 8:28).

The disciples met Spiritism in the form of sorcery.

> But there was a certain man, called Simon, which beforetime in the same city used sorcery, and bewitched the people of Samaria, giving out that himself was some great one
> (Acts 8:9).

In another case Paul and Barnabas found devil possession in the form of a false prophet.

> And when they had gone through the isle unto Paphos, they found a certain sorcerer, a false prophet, a Jew, whose name was Bar-jesus (Acts 13:6).

Devil possession takes many forms. We often associate it especially with the situation in primitive and pagan cultures, and certainly Satan has used it dramatically in some of those areas. But in the early Adventist Church there were evidences of such manifestations among the people. J. N. Loughborough, in his book, *The Rise and Progress of Seventh-day Adventists,* attests to these manifestations among early Adventists.

> There was in our company a sister, Mrs. Riggs, who seemed to be in deep trial of mind, but by the closest questioning she could not be induced to disclose the cause of her grief. Mrs. White told her the Lord had revealed to her the cause of all

Spiritism and Devil Possession

this sadness. She said, "I was shown that after you retire for the night, and extinguish the light, there appears to you what looks like an old woman dressed in black, and it terrifies you. This apparition tells you that if you tell anybody she will choke you to death. When you are in the presence of your sisters, you think you will tell them about it, and have them join you in a season of prayer that the Lord may rebuke this, which you regard as a work of Satan, which it really is. It is from the same source as the rapping spirits. The cause of your distress and staring into vacancy in the presence of your sisters is that you fear to tell them of your trial, lest the spirit carry out its threat, and take your life. Sister Riggs, I have been shown that if you take your position against this power, and have the brethren pray for you, it will be rebuked, and you will never be troubled with it again."

Mrs. Riggs did not at that time say whether this was so or not, but a few days after, as Mrs. White called at the house of Mr. Orton, she found several of the brethren present, and also this Mrs. Riggs. Mrs. White said to her, "Now, Sister Riggs, this is a good time for you to take your position against that spirit which is troubling you, and we will unite in prayer for you." The sister began to say, "It is so," but only succeeded in saying the words, "It is," when she began to struggle as though trying to extricate herself from the grasp of some strong person. She turned black in the face, as though indeed she was choking to death. Finally she cried out, "Pray." Those present immediately engaged in a season of prayer for her, and as they prayed, victory came. Mrs. Riggs rebuked this evil spirit in the name of the Lord, and was very happy

(J. N. Loughborough, *The Rise and Progress of Seventh-day Adventists*, p. 173–174).

There was another experience of Spiritism while Sister White was living in Australia.

Another matter arose in 1897 that occupied Daniells in an incident for which he relied heavily on Mrs. White's advice. She wrote to him about a canvasser, N. A. Davis [the letter is not extant], asking Daniells to deal kindly with him. Daniells promised to help him, knowing something of his activities since the 1894 Ashfield camp meeting. He explained to Mrs. White that recent reports about Davis borrowing money forced him to believe that he was a swindler, but, wrote Daniells, "I feel I must have more counsel from you before I can take another step in his case." She wrote a letter to Davis, sent it to Daniells and asked him to read it to Davis. On his return from Adelaide Daniells broke his journey at Ballarat, Victoria, and read the letter to Davis while they took a walk together. Davis confessed that for ten years he had been under the control of a lying spirit who had a white beard, wore a turban, and claimed to be an oriental from Tibet. The spirit, he said, would often terrorize him at night and threaten to kill him. That evening after dinner, Daniells prayed earnestly with Davis and his wife and the spirit left Davis. Later in his letter of explanation and thanks to Mrs. White, Daniells said: "I am very glad for the instruction you gave me to deal very kindly and patiently with him. I am glad you referred me to the statements of Jude 21–25. . . . The experience was of great value to me. I have always shrunk from meeting the devil in that form, and have dreaded the idea of having to rebuke Satan. But when I saw how the mention of the name Christ in living faith broke the power of the enemy . . . I received new impressions in regard to meeting the power of the enemy. . . . How glad I am that we have a Saviour, who had met Satan and conquered him. In Christ we need not fear"

(*Spectrum,* Volume 18, Number 5).

Russell has seen many of the spiritualistic manifestation of the Eastern religions during his ministry in the Far East.

Colin, while president of West Indies College, faced three young teenaged girls who were caught in Spiritism. The names are changed but the events are reported in brief as they occurred.

Valerie had just completed her high school years and was planning to become a college student at West Indies College in Jamaica, working during the summer at the college. Valerie had spent a number of hours with Colin, talking of the voices that she was hearing and their message for her to destroy herself. One day she walked into his office and started to talk. When Colin was talking to her, suddenly he noticed her eyes glaze. She stood up like a robot, marched out of his office and walked to the young ladies' dormitory. Colin immediately alerted the dean of women, who, a few minutes later, called desperately for help, telling him that Valerie was creating havoc in her room. On the way down

Colin asked the dean of men and the chairman of the Religion Department to come with him. In her room, Valerie's eyes were fixated upon the ceiling. Nevertheless she was ripping to shreds anything of a religious nature—books, magazines, and hymnbooks. Yet she neatly placed in a suitcase all the non-religious objects. She made no mistakes.

Without warning Valerie suddenly dashed out of the room. As the four searched desperately for her, they found her standing by a small mandarin tree near the young mens' dormitory. Colin walked up to her but initially there was not the slightest indication that she even noticed him or heard his words. As Colin prayed for God to release her, her eyes began to focus and she again came back to reality. When Colin asked her where she had been, she told him that she had come from his office, obviously totally unaware of what had happened in her room. When taken back to her room she was horrified to see the terrible state of the room and with pathetic voice asked, "Did I do that?"

As the four faculty members talked with her suddenly her eyes glazed again and she made another dash for the door. But this time she was grabbed and it took all the power of the four to wrestle her back to her bed, with the dean of men pinning her on one shoulder and Colin on the other, and the dean of women holding her legs down. At this point the chairman of the Religion Department began to pray in the name of the Lord for the release of this young woman. Her body convulsed like the waves of an ocean, leaving huge globules of perspiration on her forehead, then a great period of quiescence with deep exhausted breathing followed. But she had been delivered. In the more than two and one half years of Colin's continued stay at West Indies College, there was never an incident again involving this young lady.

In the case of the other girls, the ending was not in victory. Freda had come to the academy as a fifteen year old. She had been a popular singer on Jamaican television, but more tragically she had been steeped in Spiritism. As a youngster from the age of twelve she had been used to run ganga [marijuana] from the countryside for men who were transporting it to the United States. She particularly became fond of the nineteen-year old young man for whom she was working and "fell in love with him." But shortly afterward he was shot dead in Florida, leaving her devastated.

At this point she attended the most exclusive women's high school in Kingston. Some of the other girls, learning of her terrible grief, assured her that they could put her in touch with this departed man. They took her to a seance where an intermediatory spirit put her in touch with the "spirit" of the man who had died. But somehow in the strange twist of devil possession, she fell in love with this intermediate spirit named Jim. She had also been introduced to the ouija board at the school and later was to claim that ninety percent of the girls in that school would not so much as take an examination without consulting the ouija board.

But the first school week of prayer in the fall of the year she made a strong commitment to the Lord and publicly burned the ouija board and other materials she had brought to the college. She seemed to be doing very well, but after the Christmas break it was clear that something had changed. She had returned to her home territory of Kingston and no doubt had again reassociated with some of her friends of the past.

Shortly after her return, Colin received a frantic call from the principal of the academy for help, Freda was acting in an extraordinary manner. As Colin went to the basement of the school he saw and heard miracles take place. By this time there were a number of faculty present. Suddenly Freda reached back and desperately attempted to destroy the Bible that was on the principal's desk. Every time she was asked to call upon the name of Jesus in a defiant tone she would say, "Jim."

Suddenly her voice changed to a deep guttural male voice which said, "Leave her alone. She's mine." One of the faculty said, "No, she belongs to Jesus. She gave her heart to him," only to hear the bloodcurdling response: "But I got her back." Later she was to recite for perhaps three to five minutes an unbelievable non-stop list of Egyptian names and places.

The Academic Dean of the college decided to take her home to his place to see if he could help her pray it through. After a couple of weeks he felt she was doing a little better and persuaded the faculty to take her back.

Not long after that Colin was standing with the dean of men just prior to the commencement of the prayer meeting on a Wednesday evening when he heard the most bloodcurdling scream. Racing around the other side of the chapel he saw a great congregation of students. Breaking through he found a girl, Jean, on the concrete parapet. There was no sign of blood but the screaming continued. Colin had to shout to find anyone who had seen what had happened. Singling out two young ladies who said they had seen what had taken place, he got basically the same story from each. Jean had been sitting in chapel, she had stood up, started to walk out, then ran diving head-first into the concrete. But there were no bruises, no sign of any injury whatsoever.

Eventually, with the screaming still continuing, he had to get some of the strong young men to carry this girl to the girls' dormitory. The screaming was so penetrating that Colin's wife who had not yet left for prayer meeting thought the screaming was on her doorstep even though her house was 300 yards away from the girls' dormitory.

Suddenly Freda appeared and started to shout, "Get away from her. Leave her alone." Colin had no sooner asked that Freda be taken out of the way when suddenly she, too, started screaming with Jean. There was nothing that could be done. The student body was terrorized by the experience. While the girls were separated in the dormitory, one end from the other, as soon as one would start to scream, the other would scream. Eventually nine ordained ministers were praying for the deliverance of these young ladies, but nothing happened, until Colin had to say, "There is no point; they clearly are holding onto the things of Satan."

In the end, at one o'clock in the morning, a physician had to inject the girls with a strong narcotic. In spite of this, early the next morning they were both awake again. As Colin, with the Academic Dean, approached Freda he demanded what she had in the room that belonged to Satan. She claimed, Nothing; but Colin would not accept such an answer and eventually she gave him two books. One book was called *The Occult in Salem,* dealing with the witchcraft in Salem, Massachusetts and the second book was a medical journal. Its cover story was "Devil Doctors in the United States." Colin knew why it was impossible for her to be freed because, like Jean, she was holding firm to the spiritualistic emblems to which Satan had led her.

When, the next night, they started screaming in unison again, there was only one decision to make—to send them home; Freda to Kingston and Jean to her home in New York City. The difference between their circumstances and Valerie's was clear. Valerie had a genuine desire to separate herself from whatever had led her into these spiritualistic practices. On the other hand, neither Freda nor Jean had made such a commitment and therefore they held to these devilish practices.

Myriads of missionaries can attest to the strength of devil possession and its commonplace practices in the world and even among those who claim to be Seventh-day Adventists. But there are others who can attest that such manifestations are also to be found among those who claim to be Seventh-day Adventist in the first-world countries.

As we come to the end of time, it is to be expected that there will be more of these overt manifestations, even among those who claim to be Seventh-day Adventists. Satan often wins these battles through curiosity, especially that of young people, as they crave to find out what is taking place. But God is calling upon us to avoid experimenting with seances, ouija boards, necromancy, hypnotism, mind-control, and all forms of satanic practices. There is no safety in such curiosity. We need to avoid deliberate confrontations and associations with Satan under all circumstances.

12

Spiritism and the New Age

The New Age is nothing more than ancient humanistic paganism. Elements of it can be seen back in the time of Babylon, but it reached a zenith during the golden age of Greece. Humanism is simply the concept that man, within himself, has the answer to every human need; that he is able to establish the perfect world. It fits beautifully with the evolutionary doctrine of more modern times that man is evolving to a higher and better society. In spite of the obvious evidences that man is becoming more and more perverse, myriads still cling to the thought that through the acceptance and education of humanistic principles, the whole sin problem of the world will be solved by man, himself. The concept is based upon a fallacious view that man is innately good, or, as the Greeks would have put it, that the soul is innately good. Greek philosophy posited that man is a dichotomy of a perfect, all-knowing soul in an evil body. The concept is found in many psychological theories of today. For example, it underscores the concept of non-directed therapy as propounded by Carl Rogers.

Socrates certainly spread his doctrines, directly and through his pupils such as Plato. His dictum, "To know is to do," was built upon the fallacy that all we have to do is educate children in a natural environment and help them to explore what is right and what is truthful, and they will automatically follow these principles. One who has been a parent or a teacher surely has discovered that knowledge alone does not produce correct and moral behavior. But in spite of the obvious evidence, myriads are still content to believe that in man are the answers to all his needs; that given a clear understanding of those answers, he will follow them.

Back in the time of the renaissance there was a revival of Greek culture and therefore of these humanistic concepts. By the eighteenth century men like Jean Jacques Rousseau strongly propounded this humanistic concept. Rousseau wrote a novel, *Emile*, in which he expanded the concept that children growing up naturally, in an unpolluted country environment, would grow up to be good men. Also in the novel, Sophie was trained to be the "perfect, subservient" wife to Emile. But those who attempted to follow the philosophy of Rousseau found that all their hopes were dashed. The natural inclination of man is evil. Therefore left to his own devices, untrained, and undisciplined, his life will be one of great wickedness.

Indeed there is one extant record of a man in England who decided to raise two little girls according to the philosophy of Rousseau. He kept a careful diary and soon he was reporting the totally unrestrained behavior of these girls. He had hoped that the one who turned out the better would become his wife in adulthood, but of course he ended up marrying neither of them.

Throughout recent times this humanistic philosophy has pervaded the earth. For example, the philosophers whose theories were to be the basis that led to the French Revolution were under the influence of humanistic theorizing. Their writings sound beautiful and persuasive. But when put into practice at the time of the French Revolution, rather than leading to great love and social equality, they led to over 40,000 men and women being beheaded and hundreds of thousands losing their lives in the Napoleonic wars. Every evidence of the manifestation of humanism has led to terrible disaster.

After the French Revolution, the love relationship with humanism continued. None were more effective in continuing the myth of humanism than Karl Marx and Engels. Rather than seeing the total failure of humanism in the French Revolution, and in the revolutions that swept Europe in 1848, Karl Marx decided that it wasn't humanism that was wrong, it was the way in which the leaders of these revolutions failed to perfectly implement the principles of humanism. He wrote books that he thought were designed to bring about an earthly utopia built on humanistic principles. But they led to the great Bolshevist Revolution in Russia. After the Second World War, Communism expanded to many parts of the planet until almost half the population of the world was under its bloodstained banner. But rather than bringing the utopia, we have seen the successive dismantling of communistic states. Such philosophy led to an estimated forty million people losing their lives under the ruthless regime of Josef Stalin, and to millions of others losing their lives in other communist countries of the world.

It would be expected that with the failure of humanism down through the history of the world, somehow the concept would be grasped that humanism has no answer to the problems of the world. But today there is a humanistic thrust greater, more universal, than at any time in the history of the world. The name may be changed to New Age, but the principles are the same ancient pagan humanism. One only has to go to a bookstore and look at the section entitled "New Age" to see a conglomeration of Eastern paganism, Spiritism, humanism and satanism. That alone should be sufficient to lead men and women to reject and eschew the New Age movement.

Some have tried to put a Christian connotation upon humanism by calling it Christian humanism, but that is an anomaly, for the very nature of humanism sees man as his own savior, his own redeemer, the solution to every human problem; whereas Christianity is built upon Christ, and His answer to every human problem. One philosophy depends wholly upon man, the other depends wholly upon God. There can be no rational marriage between the two.

The whole concept of the New World Order is a New Age concept built around humanistic principles that are supposed to bring into the third millennium peace, prosperity, justice and equality for all. One thing that can be confidently predicted without any possibility of error is that the New Age movement is destined to fail miserably. It will end in the greatest catastrophe that this world has ever known. Jesus makes the issue clear.

> Without me ye can do nothing   (John 15:5).

In scripture we find the positive and only way that man can be everything that he was created to be.

> With God all things are possible   (Matthew 19:26).

The New Age underscores almost every kind of motivational philosophy today and almost every training and educational program, whether it be stress control, marriage enhancement, management, salesmanship, educational improvement, interpersonal relations, and so forth. Almost all such programs are wholly unsuitable for Christians and should thus be avoided.

The New Age is bound up with Spiritism and paganism; and more and more evidence comes to light of the strong influence of Roman Catholicism in its present-day thrust.

Some time back a special five-hour television spectacular was beamed by satellite from New York City all over the world in the cause of the New Age movement, especially in relationship to the "Save our earth" initiatives. In the program, John Denver, a well-known New Age advocate, sang the song "It's About Time." There is great significance in the first two verses of this song.

> There's a full moon over India, and Ghandi lives again.
> Who's to say you have to lose for someone else to win.
> In the eyes of all the people the look is much the same,
> For the first is just the last one, when you play a deadly game.
>
> There's a light in the Vatican window for all the world to see,
> And a voice cries in the wilderness, sometimes he speaks to me.
> I suppose I love him most of all when he kneels to kiss the land.
> With his lips upon our mother's breast, he makes his strongest stand.

It is not difficult to note that the first verse is repeating the reincarnational beliefs of Ghandi. The second shows the close connection with the Papacy and the Pope. For the New Age, along with the ecumenical movement and the charismatic movement, provides the "glue" necessary to bring about the one-world government and the one-world religion led by the pope. Few Adventists understand the deep connections.

When the great New Age conference was held in Costa Rica in June, 1989, most of the leaders were Roman Catholic, and the Roman Catholic Church gave strong support to it. You may have noticed how the New Age movement has begun to affect the theology of many in the Seventh-day Adventist Church. More and more we are listening to the specious philosophies of men, their psychologies and sociologies, with the thought that this will enable us to be better Christians, or to win souls more effectively, or bring back inactive members into the ranks of God's church. But in so doing we are just as surely going to the gods of Ekron as were the Israelites of old, for the New Age is rank paganism built upon the idolatrous principles of the pre-Christian Gentiles. Indeed the New Age has really brought together the social sciences, mind control programs, educational, health, and vocational programs. All this is done to bring about a supposed unity, but the results will be disastrous.

There is absolutely no place for the New Age movement in the Seventh-day Adventist Church. Therefore there is no place for it in the life or experience of any faithful member of the Seventh-day Adventist Church.

13

Spiritism and Entertainment

Few people stop to consider the important role of entertainment in the development of spiritualistic principles. But this was certainly not lost to the servant of the Lord who strongly associated worldly amusements with spiritualistic and satanic practices.

> Thus Satan and his angels are laying their snares for souls. They are working upon the minds of teachers and students to induce them to engage in exercises and amusements which become intensely absorbing, and which are of a character to strengthen the lower passions and to create appetites and passions that will counteract the operations of the Spirit of God upon human hearts. . . .
>
> Amusements are doing more to counteract the working of the Holy Spirit than anything else, and the Lord is grieved
> (*Counsels to Parents, Teachers, and Students*, p. 281).
>
> The desire for excitement and pleasing entertainment is a temptation and a snare to God's people, and especially to the young. Satan is constantly preparing inducements to attract minds from the solemn work of preparation for scenes just in the future. Through the agency of worldlings he keeps up a continual excitement to induce the unwary to join in worldly pleasures. . . .
>
> Satan is a persevering workman, an artful, deadly foe. . . . He has many finely-woven nets, which appear innocent, but which are skillfully prepared to entangle the young and unwary. The natural mind leans toward pleasure and self-gratification. It is Satan's policy to fill the mind with a desire for worldly amusement, that there may be no time for the question, How is it with my soul?
> (*Counsels to Parents, Teachers, and Students*, p. 325).

Sister White has special counsel against the theater. This ought to be considered very seriously in the age of television. Many Seventh-day Adventist members are spending hours daily before the television's hypnotic influence.

Spiritism and Entertainment

> Among the most dangerous resorts for pleasure is the theater. Instead of being a school for morality and virtue, as is so often claimed, it is the very hotbed of immorality. Vicious habits and sinful propensities are strengthened and confirmed by these entertainments. Low songs, lewd gestures, expressions, and attitudes, deprave the imagination and debase the morals. Every youth who habitually attends such exhibitions will be corrupted in principle. There is no influence in our land more powerful to poison the imagination, to destroy religious impressions, and to blunt the relish for the tranquil pleasures and sober realities of life than theatrical amusements. The love for these scenes increases with every indulgence, as the desire for intoxicating drink strengthens with its use. The only safe course is to shun the theater, the circus, and every other questionable place of amusement
> (*Counsels to Parents, Teachers, and Students,* pp. 334–335).

Reflecting upon this statement, surely it would be wise to have nothing to do with television. Many faithful Christians have found the wisest step is to have no television at all, for today the sensual and violent presentations on television are more vivid and more destructive than in the days when Sister White wrote these words of warning.

When we see the frivolous activities and the cheap entertainment and activities of professed believers, we can but reflect upon the terrible warnings that God has given.

> The low, common pleasure parties, gatherings for eating and drinking, singing and playing on instruments of music, are inspired by a spirit that is from beneath. They are an oblation unto Satan
> (*Counsels to Parents, Teachers, and Students,* p. 367).

Such statements link the normal entertainment common in our church gatherings with the spiritualistic principles of Satan. Indeed, they are linked with Satan-worship.

Paul, in tragic language, describes this generation of professed believers:

> Lovers of pleasure more than lovers of God; having a form of godliness, but denying the power thereof (2 Timothy 3:4–5).

A careful look at the situation in the experience of the Israelites leads us to a clear understanding that competitive games are spiritualistic in nature. If one traces the history of sports we find that they were always associated with the pagans and reached a zenith in the time of the Greeks. Having slaves to perform the so-called menial tasks of life, they did not believe in God's plan of work for the freeman. Their exercise was built upon games, all of which were designed to improve the skills of war. The pagan origin of sports, their war-like nature, their competitiveness, and the vicious rivalry often engendered by them all ought to be sufficient evidence for any perceptive Christian to steer clear of them.

When Moses was absent from the people they became restless and they exerted their influence upon the weak Aaron to mold a golden calf. It will be noted that this idolatrous worship is associated with a special form of feasting, sports and music.

> Tomorrow is a feast to the Lord. And they rose up early on the morrow, and offered burnt offerings, and brought peace offerings; and the people sat down to eat and to drink, and rose up to play (Exodus 32:5,6).

> And when Joshua heard the noise of the people as they shouted, he said unto Moses, There is a noise of war in the camp. And he said, It is not the voice of them that shout for mastery, neither is it the voice of them that cry for being overcome: but the noise of them that sing do I hear. And it came to pass, as soon as he came nigh unto the camp, that he saw the calf, and the dancing (Exodus 32:17–19).

There are many things associated with pagan practices that can be seen from this passage. One, the feasting; two, the playing of certain sports; three, the employment of wild, no doubt, pagan music; four, the practice of dancing. Doubtless, all these things they had seen in pagan Egypt and now they were lusting for the practices of the pagan nations.

Just as surely today God's church is indulging in these four abominations; the feasting, the sports-playing, the pagan music, and the dancing. It is significant to note that in Exodus 32:5 Aaron had the audacity to call it a feast unto the Lord. Today many leaders in God's church call these pagan assemblies as assemblies unto God when indeed they are an abomination unto Him.

Sister White associates this kind of practice with idolatry. Applying this experience of Israel to our day, the servant of the Lord says,

> Like Israel of old, the pleasure lovers eat and drink, and rise up to play. There is mirth and carousing, hilarity and glee. In all this the youth are following the example of the ungodly authors of some of the books that are placed in their hands for study. All these things are having their effect upon the character.
>
> Those who take the lead in these frivolities bring upon the cause a stain not easily effaced. They wound their own souls, and will carry the scars through their lifetime. The evildoer may see his sins and repent, and God may pardon the transgressor; but the power of discernment which ought ever to be kept keen and sensitive to distinguish between the sacred and the common, is in a great measure destroyed
>
> (*Counsels to Parents, Teachers, and Students*, pp. 367–368).

Later in the same book Sister White raises some very heart-searching questions.

> How much time is spent by intelligent human beings in horse racing, cricket matches, and ball playing! But will indulgence in these sports give men a desire to know truth and righteousness? Will it keep God in their thoughts? Will it lead them to inquire, How is it with my soul?
>
> (*Counsels to Parents, Teachers, and Students*, p. 456).

The idolatrous nature of sports was once vividly described by Sister White in April, 1900, on the third anniversary of the foundation of Avondale College in Australia. The students had taken an afternoon with the faculty for games which included such activities as egg and spoon race, sack race, three-legged race, potato race, and the girls had played some tennis, not on a tennis court but on the rough campus with a rope used as a "net." The young men had played a game of cricket, not on a proper cricket field, but again on the rough ground of the campus. God came to Sister White and revealed what had taken place. Here are her words:

> In the night season I was a witness to the performance that was carried on on the school grounds. The students who engaged in the grotesque mimicry that was seen acted out the mind of the enemy, some in a very unbecoming manner. A view of things was presented before me in which the students were playing games of tennis and cricket [in America it would have been tennis and softball]. Then I was given instruction regarding the character of these amusements. They were presented to me as a species of idolatry, like the idols of the nations (*Counsels to Parents, Teachers, and Students*, p. 350).

When one understands the Bible and Spirit of Prophecy approach to sports, one understands the terrible idolatry into which the Seventh-day Adventist Church has fallen. Remember, these games at Avondale College were not even intramural games; they were not played in proper conditions for sports. They were just a one-afternoon activity, but God declared it to be idolatry like the idols of the nations.

In the same passage Sister White tells us that the teachers were weighed in the balances and found wanting, and that had probation closed at that time many souls would have been lost for the kingdom. This, of course, is the whole reason for the intoxication of sports today, to lead men and women away from God and from the sober reality of preparing their lives for the coming of the Lord and for witnessing the wonderful gospel of Jesus Christ to men and women.

The tragic trend in our churches and in our schools and colleges bespeaks the widespread idolatry that is now rampant among Seventh-day Adventists. We started with pick-up games, we moved to intramurals, we moved then to playing some games between Adventist institutions, and now we have gone the full circle and have joined the leagues of the world. We are even offering scholarships to some of the better sporting performers. God must pronounce it "Abomination."

The authors both remember the very first time that a Hollywood-type film was shown by their church. We were teenagers, just after the Second World War, and the film under the auspices of the church seemed to be appropriate. It was a simple plot dealing with a German lady who had been separated from her child and the whole purpose of the story was to bring the predictable end in which she eventually found her lost child. The operators of the movie projector covered their hand over the projector so that no one would see the no doubt well-known Hollywood company that had made the film. Apparently there was one kissing scene in it and the hand went over again so that that would not be seen. But from that kind of start, today films of all sorts are shown in our churches and our educational institutions.

Remembering again the condemnation of God upon these idolatrous and satanic amusements, we have to recognize that we have moved far away from God, His way, and His righteousness. God is calling for us to educate the final generation for the finishing of the work. The training of our youth for service is a solemn and sober responsibility. As the servant of the Lord says,

> With such an army of workers as our youth, rightly trained, might furnish, how soon the message of a crucified, risen, and soon-coming Saviour might be carried to the whole world!
> (*Education*, p. 271).

Even our church papers are now advertising such amusements, unfit for those who are being called to carry the banner of the final generation to the world. For example, the Rocky Mountain Conference offered this advertisement:

> Breckenridge, Colorado, will be the site of the third annual Rocky Mountain Conference Adventist Winter Ski Festival, March 4–11, 1992. More than 600 participants are expected from all over North America for this recreational and spiritual event. Young, old, families, singles, church youth groups, academies, colleges and ski clubs are all invited. Sabbath programming includes a Friday night drama presentation, Sabbath morning worship services, Sabbath afternoon biblical snow carving contests, a concert, and more
> (*Pacific Union Recorder*, November 4, 1991).

It is clear that the kind of entertainment offered here, even that intrudes upon the Sabbath hours, is wholly unacceptable to God's men and women who are consecrated to the final generation. It represents that which God calls abomination. The drama, which is wholly condemned in the writings of the Spirit of Prophecy, and the snow carving contest, bad though it would be any day, to be held on Sabbath shows a total lack of the true principles of holy and sanctified living.

Another instance of such satanic practices came in the form of the annual banquet in a church in Northern California. We hasten to add that this is just an example of what is happening in many of our churches today.

> Annual Camino banquet featuring a magical evening with Pete McCloud. Pete McCloud is a professional speaker and award-winning entertainer using sleight of hand illusions with his talk to emphasize the points he is trying to make. He is a member of the Fellowship of Christian Magicians and performs for parties, banquets, schools, and churches. [The program was staged October 6, 1991.]

How can it be that we choose entertainment from those who are doing the very deceptive arts of Satan? Magic and magicians always were associated with idolatry and paganism in the times of the Old Testament. But this is what we bring into our church activities today. God must be dishonored.

But it takes much more than talking about these abominations in our church. It is essential for all of us to recognize that only a true call to repentance, reformation, and revival will transform men and women from these terrible satanic practices. There can be no half-hearted work done here; it must be a full-hearted presentation in the lives of God's children.

14

Spiritism and Doctrinal Deviations

The acceptance of true doctrine is central to the worship of the true God. The minister is admonished,

> Preach the word; be instant in season, out of season; reprove, rebuke, exhort with all longsuffering and doctrine
> (2 Timothy 4:2).

Paul exhorts God's people in these words:

> Holding fast the faithful word as he hath been taught, that he may be able by sound doctrine both to exhort and to convince the gainsayers (Titus 1:9).

> But speak thou the things which become sound doctrine
> (Titus 2:1).

> Till I come, give attendance to reading, to exhortation, to doctrine (1 Timothy 4:13).

> Take heed unto thyself, and unto the doctrine; continue in them: for in doing this thou shalt both save thyself, and them that hear thee (1 Timothy 4:16).

> In all things shewing thyself a pattern of good works: in doctrine shewing uncorruptness, gravity, sincerity (Titus 2:7).

> Not purloining, but shewing all good fidelity; that they may adorn the doctrine of God our Saviour in all things
> (Titus 2:10).

These are just a few of the counsels that Paul has given. There are many today who say we need to preach Christ and not doctrine. This message comes directly out of the heart of Spiritism.

> Spiritualism is now changing its form, veiling some of its more objectionable and immoral features, and assuming a Christian guise. Formerly it denounced Christ and the Bible; now it professes to accept both. The Bible is interpreted in a manner that is attractive to the unrenewed heart, while its solemn and vital truths are made of no effect. A God of love

is presented; but his justice, his denunciations of sin, the requirements of his holy law, are all kept out of sight
(*Spirit of Prophecy,* Volume 4, p. 405).

Today many are giving the love theology but they are ignoring the doctrines of the Word which are the greatest revelation of Christ and God. Indeed, of every doctrine, Christ is the center and the focus. How can we preach the Second Coming of Christ without preaching of the One who is coming in power and great glory? How can we preach the sanctuary message without preaching of the One who is our Sacrifice, our Judge, our High Priest, our Intercessor, our Advocate, our Mediator? How can we preach the Investigative Judgment without preaching of the One who will stand up for His faithful people in the judgment? How can we preach baptism without understanding the death, burial, and resurrection of Christ and the renewal that it brings to everyone who has committed his life to Christ? How can we preach the state of the dead without preaching of the One who is the Resurrection and the Life? How can we teach the commandments without recognizing that the commandments are the very expression of the character of God? How can we preach the Sabbath without preaching of the One who is our Creator, our Re-creator, and Sanctifier? How can we preach righteousness by faith without preaching of the One who imputes and imparts His righteousness to us?

But for many members, years go by and they hear nothing in the Seventh-day Adventist Church pulpits that would remotely address any of these thrilling truths. Present truth is forgotten and Satan is gaining marked inroads through the spiritualistic teachings which ignore God's justice, His denunciation of sin, and the requirements of His holy law. The representation of the Seventh-day Adventist Church surely hit an all-time low in January of 1982 when the theological representative of the Seventh-day Adventist Church signed what today has become known as the BEM document, sometimes also referred to as the Lima Text, with which most readers will probably be unfamiliar. BEM stands for Baptism, Eucharist, and Ministry. This document of the World Council of Churches is the centerpiece of their determination to bring in a one-world religion around the planet. The synopsis of the purposes of the document are these:

1. **Baptism:** to encourage all churches to make no issue of the mode of or the age at baptism. If adult consent and decision baptism is practiced by immersion, that is acceptable, as equally is infant sprinkling.

No authentic Seventh-day Adventist could accept such a proposition.

2. **Eucharist:** the term Eucharist is certainly not a Protestant term, yet at least in one church in Auckland, New Zealand, and one church in Sydney, Australia, the communion has been referred to in their church bulletin as the Eucharist. This Catholicizing of the Adventist Church is not by accident. It is a deliberate effort to bring us under the banner of the Papacy controlled by Satan.

Again, the purpose of the document is to encourage all to accept equally the various concepts, whether they be trans-substantiation, con-substantiation, or the fact that the bread and wine are symbols of the broken body and spilled blood of Jesus Christ.

When we recognize the absolutely blasphemous claims of the Roman Catholic Church, which claims that the priest is the creator of his Creator, that in the wafer he creates Christ in reality; when one considers the claims that the priest can move Christ here and there, backward and forward,* once again no earnest Seventh-day Adventist could ever accept such an abominable compromise.

3. **Ministry:** the purpose of the document is to encourage all churches to work for the unchurched but never to proselytize from other churches. The acceptance of this agreement would lead to a total capitulation from the final message which we are commissioned by our God to give to the world—the loud cry of Revelation 18:4, "Come out of her, my people, that ye be not partakers of her sins, and that ye receive not of her plagues."

Yet today we are hearing voices in the Adventist Church, ministers calling for the same ministry as these ecumenical forces in our world. "Let us work for the unchurched."

---

* See *Antichrist Is Here,* Colin and Russell Standish, 1990, chapter entitled "Blasphemous Claims"

While we cannot, of course, ignore the unchurched—we must work for them—such statements deny the critical call to work for those who have been trapped in the churches of Catholicism and fallen Protestantism. The back of the BEM document reveals a most startling statement:

> The statement published here marks a major advance in the ecumenical journey. The result of a fifty-year process of study and consultation, this text on Baptism, Eucharist, and Ministry represents a theological convergence that has been achieved through decades of dialogue, under the guidance of the Holy Spirit.
>
> Over 100 theologians met in Lima, Peru in January 1982, and recommended *unanimously* to transmit this agreed statement—the Lima Text—for the common study and official response of the churches. They represented virtually all the major church traditions: Eastern Orthodox, Oriental Orthodox, Roman Catholic, Old Catholic, Lutheran, Anglican, Reformed, Methodist, United, Disciples, Baptists, *Adventists,* and Pentecostal.
>
> The churches' response to this agreed statement will be a vital step of the ecumenical process of "reception"
>
> *(Lima Text,* emphasis ours).

It was one of the most disheartening revelations to the authors of this book to learn that Dr. Raoul Dederen, professor at the Seminary at Andrews University was the Seventh-day Adventist representative at this meeting. It could be argued that the document constituted simply a statement to which various churches were to respond. However, such would be an unacceptable answer. To consider signing (or to refrain from opposing) such a document is a gross dereliction of responsibility of a representative of the Seventh-day Adventist Church.

The document was sent to over one hundred seventy church denominations including the Seventh-day Adventist Church. Our response is in book two of the responses to the BEM document.

In reviewing this response, generally, we perceive it to be a sound response. In no wise does it support any of the obvious problems in the document. For example, the issue of baptism is stated in a manner to clearly show our allegiance to adult consent immersion baptism. We could wish however that the response of the Seventh-day Adventist church would have come out far more strongly against the whole process and the clear ecumenical goals of the BEM document.

At this time in earth's history the Seventh-day Adventist Church needs to stand clearly and unmovably for the principles of religious freedom, and pointedly expose the goals of the one-world religion, World Council of Churches, the Ecumenical movement and their connection with spiritualistic, New Age and pagan concepts. A failure to do this has opened the gate for these same concepts to come in. It seems as if a flood gate has been opened.

For example, today we see that a number of our colleges use the book, *Becoming a Master Student*. This book is wholly developed upon the New Age philosophy, and yet freshmen students are required in some of our colleges to study this book as a part of their general education requirements. But just a brief look at the book shows how totally foreign to Christianity it is, and how wholly in line with the spiritualistic self-centeredness of paganism.

> You can change your attitudes by regular practice with affirmations and visualizations
> (*Becoming a Master Student*, p. 314).

> Visualizations and affirmations can restructure your attitudes and behavior. Be clear about what you want and then practice
> (ibid., p. 315).

> "Be it" is the ultimate power process. All of the techniques in this book are enhanced by the power process. The idea is that getting what you want to *be* by what you *do* or by what you *have* is like swimming against the current. . . .

> If you can visualize where you want to be, if you can go there in your imagination, if you can *be it,* then you have set yourself up to achieve your goal. You can soon *have* and *do* what you want. This is true because, as human beings, we subconsciously create whomever we think we are (ibid. p. 322)

Even an unschooled person would know how foolish such a philosophy is. There are myriads of things that human beings cannot do, but here built upon the concept of innate goodness, upon the Greek pagan philosophy of the god within man, it would seem that man could do anything to which his imagination could aspire.

Colin very well remembers a boy in the Jewish school in which he taught back in the 1950s. This boy was a very ambitious lad, but as the oldest student in the class, he was also the least able. But he kept aspiring to be a doctor; he had a vision; he had the drive and the desire, but as one could well predict, there was no way he could fulfill such a goal. The philosophy of *Becoming a Master Student* is not only pagan, it is also the philosophy that will lead many to discouragement and failure. Young people will be inspired to imagine things that they want to do that they will never be able to achieve, and then they will wonder why.

The book becomes even worse as it develops. In a chapter entitled, "Contributing, The Art of Selfishness," it says:

> This book is about contributing to yourself, about taking care of yourself, being selfish, and filling yourself up. The techniques and suggestions in these pages focus on how to get what you want out of school and out of life. One of the results of all this successful selfishness is the capacity for contribution, for giving to others. Contributing is what is left to do when you are satisfied—filled up—and it completes the process (ibid., p. 328).

One would think that even an atheist or an agnostic would see the fallacy of such a statement. Both the authors have studied psychology, especially in the area of learning and habituation. We know full well that learning one kind of habit does not stimulate the opposite habit. How can someone whose whole motivation is selfish at some point of time suddenly become selfless? It just doesn't work that way. Indeed, selfishness is such a bottomless pit that it can never be satiated. Therefore, there will be no contributing. What we have here is a foolish humanistic principle built upon egocentricity, the principle of Satan, not the principle of God. Indeed, for eternity only one motivation existed and that was selflessness, until the selfish ambitions of Lucifer began to develop. It was Lucifer who brought into the universe the concept of selfishness. Both selflessness and selfishness are powerful motivators. When sin and sinners are destroyed eternally, once again, for the endless ages of eternity, only one motivation will exist—selflessness.

Spiritism and Doctrinal Deviations

One can hardly imagine that any Seventh-day Adventist college professor would consider for five seconds subjecting our students to such an anti-Christian book, let alone teaching it from a positive perspective. Some may argue that we can take the good that is in the book. But to place eighteen-year-olds in front of such a book and expect them to discriminate wisely and clearly between what is truth and what is error, is a task wholly beyond the ability of most of the youth of the Seventh-day Adventist Church today. Our burden surely is to educate these young people to give their lives selflessly in the service of God and man, not for the egocentric goals of their own satisfaction and selfish desires.

One wonders how it came about that we see this kind of situation in our church today. With the willingness among many of our church laity and even church leaders today to sell out to the ecumenical band wagon , is it any wonder that every pillar of our faith is under attack, every doctrine is pluralized and every standard questioned? Only by total repentance and reformation can the Lord restore the spiritual eyesight of His church today.

15

Spiritism and Seventh-day Adventist Publications

A shock wave reached around the world when at the 1990 General Conference Session the *Ministry* magazine for August, 1990, was distributed. Many people could not believe the cover of the magazine. Colin and Russell were present at this session, Russell being a delegate from the Southeast Asia Union. Our first response was one of horror as we noted the pagan design of the cover. Later we were to discover that the painting had been commissioned, some say, for a cost of $8,000. The painting is wholly un-Adventist in every way. Indeed, more than 30 pagan, spiritualistic and Roman Catholic symbols have been found in the painting.

Presented is not the Christ of the Bible coming as King of kings and Lord of lords in power and great glory, coming with the unnumbered angels in the splendor of heaven, but rather of the cosmic christ of the New Age. The painting depicts Jesus coming to the earth, totally out of harmony with the clear testimony of the Word of God.

> Then we which are alive and remain shall be caught up together with them in the clouds, to meet the Lord in the air: and so shall we ever be with the Lord (1 Thessalonians 4:17).

Among many pagan representations in what is our premier magazine for ministers, both for Adventists and non-Adventists, are clear depictions of spirits. The lost are seen in a burning inferno, writhing in agony; wholly out of character with the fact that the destruction of the wicked does not take place until a thousand years after the resurrection of the saints. Skeletons are seen flying through the air, draped in cloth. The rainbow of the New Age is in clear view. Christ's left hand presents the papal symbol of the thumb and two outer fingers curled and the semi-V-shape of the other two fingers.

During the life of Ellen White there was an attempt to put into one of her publications a picture showing Christ with this papal symbol. She demanded that they get rid of it and expressed her total consternation that her editors would have such little insight.

I wish to say to you that I am sadly disappointed in the cuts prepared for such a book as the Life of Christ [*The Desire of Ages*]. I consider that if Brother A accepts such figures that his eye and taste has lost its cunning. You cannot expect me to be pleased with such productions. Look at these figures critically, and you must see that they are either made from Catholic designs or Catholic artists. The picture of Mary has a man's face, the representation of Christ with the two fingers prominent, while the others are closed, is wholly a Catholic sign and I object to this. I see but very little beauty in any of the faces, or persons. There is the scenery of nature, landscape scenery, that is not as objectionable, but I could never rest my eyes upon the face pictures without pain.

I would much prefer to have no pictures than representations that are not representations, but disfigurements of the true. This is my opinion. Where is the discerning eye? Better pay double price, or treble, and have pictures, if pictures must be had, that will not pervert facts. I wish there had not been an attempt to make one representation, but send out the book and let it make a place for itself. I call these faces in the pictures and scenes so poorly represented that it is a perversion of the facts.

If this is A's work, I cannot accept him as a designer. And if he can accept such pictures I cannot respect or honor his judgment. Do not spoil my book by disfigurements which lower the facts and the matters they represent. Brother A needs the sanctification of the senses to understand the spirituality of truth. He may study European artistic skill, but there will be seen in nearly all designs the Catholic features
(Letter 81A, December 20, 1897).

Over many years Seventh-day Adventists have been greatly blessed by Arthur Maxwell's *Bible Story*. Yet in his opening pages of Volume 1, it brings forth a mysticism that is wholly unfit for a Seventh-day Adventist publication.

Many years ago I read a story about a boy who picked up a strange little object on the street. It was shaped like a horseshoe and had a mysterious name written on it. The boy tried to pronounce the name, but failed. He tried again and again. Then one day as he said the word a different way the object began to grow in his hand. It became bigger and bigger, until at last the horseshoe was as big as a doorway. He stepped through it and found himself in a foreign country, far across the sea. Day by day, using his horseshoe, he visited all sorts of strange places. Then he thought he would like to see how people lived long ago. So as he whispered the magic word to the horseshoe he said he would like to visit Rome in the days of the Caesars—and, presto, there he was!

Of course, it was only a made-up story, but it does give us an idea. Would you like to go and see what the world was like back in the very beginning of time? You would? All right. Let's imagine that there is an archway through which we can pass and travel back across the years.

Steady now. Careful. Now we are going through it. Everything around us is fading away. Chairs, table, carpets, radio set, are all disappearing. Faces are growing dim. Lights are going out. It is getting darker and darker.

Swiftly we speed back across the years. It's like being in a rocket plane. We streak over hundreds and thousands of years in a moment. Past the time when Jesus lived on earth
(Arthur Maxwell, *Bible Stories,* vol. 1).

Surely such imaginary concepts are inimical to the Bible and its story. It is sad that a series of books that has otherwise been such a blessing starts with such an imaginative theme.

At the General Conference Annual Council held in Perth October, 1991, readers of the *South Pacific Record* were shocked to recognize that pagan and spiritualistic dances of aborigines were featured as part of the program at the Annual Council. God called us to take the gospel to these people so that these paganistic practices might be eradicated, but it would seem that by such demonstrations at the Annual Council we were giving credence to the validity of these pagan practices. God initially called us to an entirely and wholly higher calling than this.

Perhaps an even greater shock was the distribution by the Potomac Adventist Book Center in the fall of 1991, of its "Fall into the Holiday Sale." While it has been stated that this catalogue had been prepared by a non-Seventh-day Adventist book distributor, it was wholly repugnant to the Adventist message. Can you imagine the advertising of such compact disk records as "Carmen, Commissioned and the Christ Church Choir—*Shakin' the House."*? One doesn't have to have too much imagination to decide what kind of music is on this record. Neither is too much imagination required to see that this record is wholly unacceptable in an Adventist Book Center. The brochure details some of the featured singles on the record: "The Same God," "Celebrate Jesus," "Sunday's on the Way!!"

Equally objectionable is another one of the CD records, "The Katina Boyz, Smooth R and B [rhythm and blues] harmonies with a danceable beat!" What abominations in the house of the Lord!

How can it be that there could be such a lack of discernment as to put out such a brochure? One whole page is given over to fiction, including a book about the Queen of Sheba. One would have to have a lot of imagination and fiction to fill out a full book dealing with her life. But even more objectionable was a book entitled *Children In the Night* and its description, "a masterful epic fantasy of good versus evil in a subterranean world of perpetual night. A gripping tale of two heros seeking the powers and mysteries of the light. Many layers of spiritual depth." How could we advertise such a book?

Another full section dealt with self-help. One doesn't need to have much to do with the New Age movement to identify this section with New Age thinking: the concept of the god within; the concept that we have the ability to solve our own problems.

Yet another full page was given over to humor. How can it be that we can sell books about trivial humor at the end of time? One, *McPherson's Marriage Album,* states, "The funniest, most outrageous and realistic book on marriage to come along in a long time! Get ready for a high-voltage shock of humor." How can it be that Seventh-day Adventists could even consider selling such a book? Another is a comic strip about the forty years of the Children of Israel in the wilderness. This tragic experience was anything but humorous. The last book advertised, *101 Things to do During a Dull Sermon,* "A how-to spoof of many creative ways to survive those unbearably dull sermons!"

One could hardly believe that God had called the Seventh-day Adventist Church to be the final church to take the message of truth and salvation to the world. How can it be that we can be caught in such a worldly trend? Indeed the whole sixteen-page brochure seems to have only one book published by a Seventh-day Adventist press.

We are people of prophecy, and yet only one prophetic book is offered, *Major Bible Prophecies,* by John F. Walvoord. Professor Walvoord is one of the leading rapturist theologians in America today. How could we possibly promote a book by a man who is gripped by the futuristic concepts and false view of the secret rapture?

It is not difficult to see the domination of the New International Version of the Bible, which for perceptive Adventists and many non-Adventist Christians, is a perversion of the true Bible that God has preserved through the Eastern Syriac text, the basis of all Protestant Bibles during the Reformation.

Advertised are the *NIV Young Discoverist Bible,* the *Psalty's Kids Bible, NIV;* the *Adventure Bible, NIV, The Life Application Bible, NIV; Women's Devotional Bible, NIV; Closer Walk New Testament, NIV;* the *NIV Study Bible;* the *NIV Thin Line Bible;* the *NIV Serendipity Bible.* There were some advertisements for the *King James Bible* for which we were grateful.

Surely God's church is under fearful attack, not from without, but from within. Men and women who are hirelings, who are wolves in sheep's clothing, are bringing distortions and deviations to God's precious truth. We need to pray most earnestly that God will take things into His own hands and destroy the abominations so prevalent in God's remnant church today.

16

Spiritism and the Health Work

From very early times in the history of the development of the Seventh-day Adventist Church, the health message has played a prominent role. It has been referred to as "the right arm of the message," "the entering wedge." It has formed the basis of leading many men and women to a knowledge of Christ, to His salvation, and to the three angels' messages. It has been the basis of establishing many institutions of healing around the world. However, as the years have passed, more and more our emphasis has been upon acute care medicine rather than upon lifestyle changes and simple health education. While no one is denying the need for acute care medicine, that was never meant to be our major focus in medical missionary work.

Even more alarming has been the introduction of permissive abortion into some of our hospitals, and the intrusion of Eastern mystical medicine in some of them, including acupuncture.* It cannot be denied that this is a major trend within the world and that more and more people are seeking the solutions of alternative medicine built upon paganistic principles.

In its cover story, November 4, 1991, *Time* magazine explored New Age alternative medicine. While admitting that some of the medical practices associated with the New Age are believable, many of them are bizarre. The magazine identified four major forms of New Age medicine; Lifestyle, Botanical, Manipulative/hands-on, and Mind over Matter. Some facets of these have merit. Nevertheless, almost inevitably such practices are mixed with pagan spiritualistic concepts and ideas.

Under the heading of Lifestyle, the magazine included such forms of treatment as Macrobiotics in which, in the dietary and health discipline program there is the attempt to balance the yin [passive energy] and yang [active energy]. This, of course, comes from the mystical Chinese balancing of the yin and the yang. The

---

*See *Two Be One* by Ernest Steed, available from Hartland Publications.

Chinese have identified over 270 of the polar opposites (e.g. heat and cold; good and evil; male and female; light and dark) and some of them are used within the medical field.

Ayurvedic Medicine is a system of Indian treatments more than 4000 years old, in which, while using no-doubt-valuable herbs and massage, they depend upon body types for detailing the kind of treatment that should be given. And third under Lifestyle is included Holistic Medicine. This is a treatment built in some ways upon conventional medicine but emphasizing lifestyle and psychological factors in the treating of the whole person. Very frequently it, too, is intermingled with pagan philosophy.

Under the heading of Botanical are included Aromatherapy, the use of essential oils from plants and flowers in massage and in the treatment of skin or for inhalation therapy; Medicinal Herbalism —treating illness with plant-derived potions. In many of the Asiatic cultures not only are herbs used but also animal products such as ground horns, tusks, and other products.

Third, Homeopathy, which involves treating disease with tiny doses of natural substances that, in large quantities, would cause the same symptoms as the ailment, is advocated.

The third category is Manipulative/hands-on. In it are included such treatments as Reflexology, manipulating areas of the feet to affect the rest of the body; Rolfing, deep and sometimes painful massage to realign the body; Shiatsu, a Japanese therapy using pressure points; Alexander technique, training to improve poor posture and therapy to alleviate pain; Chiropractic, manipulation of the spine to relieve back ache and many other ailments; Acupressure, using fingers instead of needles in a technique similar to acupuncture; Acupuncture, an ancient Chinese method of easing pain by inserting fine needles at specific points that are said to relate to a particular part of the body.

The fourth category is Mind over Matter. Color healing— shining colored lights on the body to alter the vibrations or aura of the body. Crystal healing—using "healing energy" from quartz and other minerals to effect healing. Bioenergetics—an exchange of energy between patient and therapist. Usually the concept is that the energy of the therapist is transmitted to the weakened patient. Guided imagery—therapy is used in which the patients are encouraged to envision their own immune system battling disease. Hypnotherapy—using hypnosis through suggestion while the patient is in a trance-like state to relieve pain, to spread healing or indeed to perform operations. Bio-feedback—this technique utilizes various machines to help people to control involuntary functions, such as heart rate, circulation and tension spots.

Unfortunately many Seventh-day Adventists have been drawn to a greater or lesser extent into this New Age medicine, often reacting against the normal allopathic form of medicine, built upon the pill, the needle and the knife. As people have sought toward more natural forms of remedies, often they have innocently and unwittingly been drawn into the practice of spiritualistic medicine. The use of manipulations and of herbal remedies have been enough to convince them that this is a methodology of God, one which eschews drugs, but in reality they are following the pathway of Satan.

God's natural remedies are first and foremost built upon lifestyle change using the eight God-given remedies—a vegetarian diet, regular moderate exercise, the free use of pure water, the moderate exposure to sunshine, temperance, fresh clean air, good regular rest habits, and above all, genuine contentment through faith and trust in God. Other methods may have some of these characteristics, but Seventh-day Adventists need to be extraordinarily careful not to assume that everything under the guise of natural remedies is a method of God. When we learn of Seventh-day Adventists using crystal power to help in healing, we know that there is a great blindness among some of our people, for this certainly comes out of the mystical medicine of the Eastern religions. It is spiritualistic.

Of deepest concern has been the number of Seventh-day Adventists who are reading more and more books written by spiritists. Some are studied in our schools and colleges. One of the most deadly books available, studied by large numbers of Adventists in the health and ministerial profession, is Elizabeth Kubler-Ross', *On Death and Dying*. This book was written by a woman who is an avowed spiritist. She was born the first of three triplets in Switzerland. It is said that she was delivered by an obstetrician who was an amateur clairvoyant. Holding her up he said, "This one is going to be a pathfinder in this world." And indeed she has been, but for spiritistic concepts. She is probably the number one "expert" on the issue of death and dying today. Her books have been used in Adventist colleges in the training of nurses. They have been used in the training of chaplains, and significant numbers of our already-trained nurses have been sent to in-service training programs built upon her spiritistic philosophy. So many of our people have been trained in her techniques and ways that it is very possible that the medical work will be in the vanguard of thrusting Spiritism into the Seventh-day Adventist Church.

Surely the Bible and the Spirit of Prophecy have such wonderful counsel on how we are to deal with the sick and the dying and how to comfort them and lead them to Christ, that we do not need to go to a spiritist to discover these techniques. The Scripture tells us to comfort one another with the words contained in its pages (1 Thessalonians 4:18).

Many people have also been greatly alarmed by the Breathe-Free stop-smoking program sponsored by our Health Department. This program is built largely upon the new age philosophy. There are myriads of people in the world at large who are familiar with these kinds of techniques. But God has given us a better plan. The Breathe-Free program is unworthy of Seventh-day Adventists. First presented in 1985 by Narcotics Education Incorporated, it presents a program that is almost devoid of spirituality. Only an occasional word from Paul is mentioned at the bottom of the pages. The following are the "16 weapons to kill an urge." Many may be good principles in themselves, but without the power of Christ they are simply human tools. "1. Drink a glass of water or fruit juice. 2. Take five deep breaths. (Ease into these so as not to hyperventilate.) 3. Take a walk. 4. Do light calisthenics. 5. Do stretching and relaxation exercises. 6. Count backward starting from 100. 7. Work on a hobby. 8. Brush your teeth with a mint toothpaste. 9. Take a warm shower followed by a cool shower, then rub the body gently with a washcloth. 10. Chew on carrot or celery sticks. 11. Choose unhulled sunflower seeds to shell and eat. 12. Chew sugarless gum. 13. Call a partner for help. 14. Drink a glass of milk. 15. Repeat the affirmation 'I love being free of smoking.' 16. Look at your watch and postpone giving in for at least one minute, then start another minute and another for at least five minutes. Success comes one step at a time."

It is claimed that no urge can survive all 16 steps. It is our belief that many people have found that their urge has all too easily survived these 16 steps. There is not one word about divine power, or about the role of prayer in gaining victory. We are not in this world to present humanistic, New Age, paganistic principles. We are here to present the true gospel of Jesus Christ, to show the way to salvation. We surely believe that

> With God all things are possible (Matthew 19:26).

That promise is a promise of victory over tobacco addiction. While some of the principles that are outlined in the Breathe-Free program are good principles and certainly worthy of being taught, they are not the primary basic principles of victory. The New Age can be seen in many other aspects of it. For example, in a section entitled "Self Image" it says,

> The belief I hold about myself sets the boundaries of what I can and cannot accomplish:
> 1. I can when I believe I can.
> 2. My self image is not a permanent structure in my mind.
> 3. I will visualize myself as a non-smoker.
> 4. I will begin to be free from smoking.

Anyone even slightly familiar with the New Age will realize the New Age language and the concept of the god within. "I can when I believe I can." This is the old idea of Socrates, that "to know is to do," but indeed God cannot work through such pagan errors. What we are presenting is a program unfit for those who would want the special spiritual principles that God has presented to us.

As step by step, more of these pagan principles are introduced into our health and temperance work, less will they be avenues through which men and women will be led to God and to the kingdom of heaven. We need to use God's methods and His way of healing, and not only will the physical healings be significantly increased, but also the spiritual healings. After all it is only to be expected that we cannot rely upon God to heal through satanic methodology. The power of the Divine can only work through the principles that God has given us.

When we realize that some of the forms of psychotherapy used in our hospitals, including hypnotherapy, are likewise of satanic origin, there is a great and urgent need for us to reevaluate and come back to God's way of presenting the wonderful health message built upon His true principles of restoration. In so doing, the health message and the medical missionary work will truly become the right arm of the message.

17
Spiritism and Celebration

Our first intimation of the movement now referred to as the "Celebration" movement within the Adventist Church goes back to the beginning of the 1980s when a pastor Eion Giller began what some people thought was an unusually Pentecostal type of worship form in the Hillview Church near Avondale College. Of course this association with the Pentecostal movement was denied, but nevertheless there were some of the evidences of it: the expressive activities commonly associated with that movement.

The next alarm was sensed by Colin when, on a tour of Europe in 1987, he was told of charismatic Adventists in France and then met about a dozen of them when the Hartland Bible Conference was being held in the Central Church in Rome. It was at that point that we wrote the chapter on Pentecostalism in the book, *Keepers of the Faith,* and in so doing we were able to get a warning out prior to the movement becoming an established movement within the Seventh-day Adventist Church.

But with the introduction of such churches as the Colton Church in the Southeastern Conference, and the Milwaukie Church, Portland, in the Oregon Conference, and the Buffalo Church in the New York Conference (by the way, initialy under the leadership of Dr. Eion Giller), and of the Cherrybrook Church in Sydney, it was clear that not a small effort was going to be made to bring the elements of the charismatic movement and its sister, Pentecostalism, into the church.

We were alarmed when church leaders at the General Conference level were to repeatedly declare they could not evaluate this form of worship; that they had to wait and see, for they did not have sufficient information to make a decision. It would seem that such was rather a means of allowing the movement to develop to such an extent that there would be no way of turning it back. Those with spiritual discernment saw from the very beginning that this was nothing short of the Pentecostal and spiritualistic movement that we as a church had fought against constantly over the decades. But now it was becoming more and more a part of the church. The usual denials began to flood in when churches began to move in this direction.

The pastors were urging their churches toward Celebration services, while assuring them it wasn't Pentecostal or charismatic, but those who looked at what was taking place had not the slightest doubt that this was the Pentecostal movement being subtly and not-so-subtly introduced into the Seventh-day Adventist Church. Eventually, numerous churches began to be pressured in this direction. Some eagerly accepted this form of "worship"; others with some reservations accepted it. Still others were forced into it with many of the members clear on what was taking place, yet apparently impotent to do anything about it. The tragedy is that so many leaders, even perhaps somewhat opposed to it, keep denying the extent of this movement. There are hundreds of Seventh-day Adventist churches that have started on the pathway of the charismatic movement. Some have not reached the maturity that some of the early ones have, but they certainly have begun the pathway and we can be certain that Satan will bring them more and more into the full-fledged charismatic movement as he is able.

The whole presentation has been subtle. Colin overheard a dialogue at the General Conference session where men who were obviously supportive, and maybe leaders in the charismatic movement, were stating that the word "Celebration" had now acquired a negative connotation and that perhaps we should not use the term. This, of course, was meant to derail the efforts of faithful Adventists from identifying the charismatic movement when it came into the church. But no matter whether it is called Celebration or not, it is still the intrusion of Satan's charismatic movement. Leaders and laity alike should have been forewarned. The counsel is clear.

> The things you have described as taking place in Indiana, the Lord has shown me would take place just before the close of probation. Every uncouth thing will be demonstrated. There will be shouting, with drums, music, and dancing. The senses of rational beings will become so confused that they cannot be trusted to make right decisions. And this is called the moving of the Holy Spirit.

> The Holy Spirit never reveals itself in such methods, in such a bedlam of noise. This is an invention of Satan to cover up his ingenious methods for making of none effect the pure, sincere, elevating, ennobling, sanctifying truth for this time. Better never have the worship of God blended with music than to use musical instruments to do the work which last January was represented to me would be brought into our camp meetings (Selected Messages, Book 2, p. 36).
>
> I will not go into all the painful history; it is too much. But last January the Lord showed me that erroneous theories and methods would be brought into our camp meetings, and that the history of the past would be repeated. I felt greatly distressed. I was instructed to say that at these demonstrations demons in the form of men are present, working with all the ingenuity that Satan can employ to make the truth disgusting to sensible people; that the enemy was trying to arrange matters so that the camp meetings, which have been the means of bringing the truth of the third angel's message before multitudes, should lose their force and influence. . . .
>
> The Holy Spirit has nothing to do with such a confusion of noise and multitude of sounds as passed before me last January. Satan works amid the din and confusion of such music, which, properly conducted, would be a praise and glory to God. He makes its effect like the poison sting of the serpent
> (Ibid., p. 37).

It will be noted from these statements that this movement is not under the power of the Holy Spirit, but under the power of another spirit—Satan. Therefore it is only right that faithful Adventists do not attend such churches. Our counsel is that such members look for churches where the pastors preach present truth and where they have the stirring, soul-searching messages that God has designed for this time, with the inspiring hymns of dedication, and they teach the members to lovingly serve their fellow men and train them to witness of the great message of salvation.

It is of the greatest danger for us to go deliberately into Satan's territory. Neither one of the authors is willing to attend, knowingly, a Celebration church because of the knowledge that these churches are of Satan. We should not even allow curiosity to lead us in that direction. If Celebration is coming to your church, you have a responsibility to speak out, to urge and to counsel. But if there is no response to your counsel, and the majority of the people are determined to go with it, or lock-step follow the recommendations of the pastor in that direction, you have no alternative but to leave that church and to look for another place to worship. If there are no churches in the area, you are forced into a branch Sabbath School if that is possible, or even into home worships. This is not denying your membership of the Seventh-day Adventist Church. On the contrary, it is a very important indication that you will not move away from the truth and that you are being a faithful Seventh-day Adventist.

Those who are parents of children must be especially careful. They have a responsibility not to allow their children to go to such services, for they may be led away from salvation under the influence of Satan. Colin had the tragic experience the Sabbath before Christmas, 1990, to attend with his wife and family a church in Perth, Australia. The children were sent to the Primary and Kindergarten Sabbath School respectively. You can imagine Colin's and his wife, Cheryl's, consternation when the children of these divisions gave special music and they sang a rock Christmas carol with much jumping about and clapping and celebration-type behavior. Of course, their children had not learned this song, but as might be expected, they were trying to do what the other children were doing. How tragic such an experience is. Parents now must carefully evaluate that the Sabbath School to which they are sending their children is a fit place for them to learn the wonderful messages of God.

In August 1989 Russell attended a church in Melbourne, Australia. He had known the church in earlier times and was surprised to find it only about one-third full.

The following week there was a transformation. The church was full. The difference was astounding. After Sabbath School a young man dressed extremely casually lounged on the lectern and invited the congregation to sing some choruses projected on a screen. After about ten minutes of singing an elder came up and made an announcement. Thereafter another ten minutes of the singing of projected choruses ensued. At this point the "pastoral prayer" was announced. For the first time it dawned on Russell that we were already twenty minutes into the "divine service" and

Spiritism and Celebration

the song leader was the young pastor. The singing, interrupted once more by a children's story and the offering, had a duration of fifty minutes. The final ten minutes of the service were devoted to a short homily by the pastor, a special item and benediction. Russell had received his first introductory lesson in Celebration.

At the conclusion of the service one senior member remarked to Russell, "It's wonderful when this young pastor comes, he brings all these young people with him and fills up our church. They come from all over Melbourne and follow him wherever he preaches." Some may have thought that these young people were being spiritually fed, but Russell concluded that they were on starvation rations.

We are spending large sums of money to train our ministers in the Celebration methodology. In the Ministries Department of the seminary there is a strong training program encouraging Celebration type services. Many of our pastors and leaders from Australia and New Zealand have been taken on tours to the United States where they not only visit the more "advanced" charismatic churches of Adventism, but they attend and dialogue with pastors from non-Adventist charismatic and Pentecostal churches. It is hard to imagine that God's sacred money could be used to train our ministers away from the great purpose of God and towards the banner of Satan.

The tragedy is that few of the laity are rising up to ask for an absolute halt. In 1991 a four-day worship seminar was held mainly for ministers in the United States. Many pastors attended it including some from Australia. There is only one answer to this. In spite of leaders frequently saying they are waiting to see the results, they are indeed supporting these changes in worship form. Do such leaders have a right to continue as the guardians of the flock? They have betrayed their trust and they have allowed their ministry to come under the power of another spirit.

Colin could not have helped but notice some of the seminars offered by the Potomac Conference in Convention '91, November 1 and 2, that were promoting New Age philosophy. For example, "What you see is what you are, Christians can use meditation and visualization for peak mental health—learn how!"

In the same set of seminars participants could attend "Batman's Action-packed perspective of Sabbath School programming. Action—one of Batman's trademarks. Today young people need to learn by *doing,* not just hearing. What is active learning and how can you use it to reach your kids? In this seminar you will hear and do activities which you can use with your Juniors, Earliteens and Youth on the following Sabbath!"

Any faithful Seventh-day Adventist will be distressed by the use of a worldly television program such as Batman as a basis for training for Sabbath School class teachers. Is it any wonder then that one of the other seminars was, "How my Sunday School can help your Sabbath School." Or that we have another seminar by a non-Adventist presenter, "Growing kids spiritually in an unspiritual world. How come young people of the Baptist Church have such strong denominational loyalty, faith and values? Why are they so much stronger than our kids?"

To every perceptive Adventist the reason is simple. We are no longer presenting the challenges of the three angels' messages to our young people; we are no longer training them in selfless service for God and man; we are presenting to them the egocentric concepts of the world, rather than the power of God. One is also alarmed to see our great university churches, whether it be Loma Linda University Church, Pioneer Memorial Church at Andrews University, or the Sligo Church at Columbia Union College, all moving at least in one service to the Celebration format.

For example, the Pioneer Memorial Church at Andrews University put out its little brochure, "Sabbath Sunburst Celebration Saturday mornings at 8:45 a.m. Come fellowship with the Son, let Him burst across your horizon. A new dimension for your Sabbaths. Praise. Music. Fellowship. The spirit of worship, the song of encounter, the simplicity of celebration. Or choose the 11:20 service and experience the grandeur of traditional worship—the same inspirational preaching at both."

With tragic clarity our young people are being thrown into the arms of Satan's counterfeit and few seem to know it. Colin was concerned at the report that he received while in Brisbane at the end of 1991, where the congregation had sung the pagan hymn, "Let us break bread together on our knees." But as the people were leaving for footwashing the pastor continued to sing, accord-

Spiritism and Celebration 109

ing to some who were witnesses there, "Let us break God together on our knees." Brother Lin Harmon made this comment, "At that juncture my wife and I segregated and went home as did some others." What a tragedy that men and women are forced to go home because of the intrusion of erroneous Catholic doctrines within the church.

Nor can one remain unmoved by the service at the La Sierra University Church the end of October, 1991. Here the program contained the ecumenical words on the front of the program, "A liturgy celebration unity in diversity." There is no such thing as unity in diversity. Unity is in truth, unadulterated and uncontaminated. After reading some good scriptures and singing some good hymns, the program tragically moved into human words. For example, "In Thee, in me," translated from the Sanskrit by Mohandas Gandhi. The pantheistic spiritualism of Gandhi came through very quickly in the words used in this liturgical service. "In Thee, in me, in all persons, there dwelleth the one God."

Any Christian knows that God does not invade humanity without their permission. Revelation 3 portrays Christ as standing at the door of our hearts and knocking, and if we open the door He will come in. But pantheism believes that God is in everything and in every human being. It was this pantheism of Kellogg that God declared to be spiritualism, and yet this liturgy could be presented. Other messages were presented from John Donne, the sixteenth century English poet, "No man is an island." *Life Together* by Dietrich Bonhoeffer, *Strength to Love* by Martin Luther King, Jr., the *Peaceable Kingdom* by Stanley Hauerwas, but strangely no words from God's end-time prophet. The folk who gave to Colin the program left when a woman danced an extended liturgical dance during the divine service hour. How can it be that God's church has fallen so far and so fully into these idolatrous practices? We are repulsed by the paganism of the Israelites and the Jews and yet we ourselves have walked headlong into the same paganistic practices.

Not only is the Celebration movement seen in the use of rock and hypnotic music, but it is seen in the entertainment that is flooding into our church with comedians holding services on Sabbath such as was held on the Friday evening at the Arco Center in Sacramento the end of October, 1991. Also "clown ministry" and "miming" are in common use today in church worship.

The spiritual becomes the profane; the holy becomes corrupted; the sanctified becomes secular. How tragic are the consequences of these activities. And yet many blindly move forward saying that this is the leading of God to help our youth stay in the church. Is it any wonder that we in the Western world are losing three-quarters of our youth from the Adventist Church? Is it any wonder that we are finding our youth growing up into self-centered, pleasure seeking young people who know not the principles of the truth and who are unready for the mighty work that God has called them to fulfill?

Now is surely a day to call our people back to true worship the worship of the God of heaven, not the worship of the false god of Satan.

18

Spiritism and Witness

Every consecrated Seventh-day Adventist has been motivated by the words of Jesus,

> And this gospel of the kingdom shall be preached in all the world for a witness unto all nations; and then shall the end come (Matthew 24:14).

They have recognized that this gospel which will be preached to the whole world is the everlasting gospel of the first angel's message.

> And I saw another angel fly in the midst of heaven, having the everlasting gospel to preach unto them that dwell on the earth, and to every nation, and kindred, and tongue, and people, saying with a loud voice, Fear God, and give glory to him; for the hour of his judgment is come: and worship him that made heaven, and earth, and the sea, and the fountains of waters (Revelation 14:6–7).

In truth, few pastors or lay people could give an adequate explanation of the everlasting gospel. Without such it would be futile for God to invest His people with the power of the latter rain, the purpose of which alone is to take this gospel to every nation, kindred, tongue and people and to proclaim and herald the return of Jesus Christ.

Thus, just as in other areas of our church, we have resorted more and more to pagan concepts to try to spread the gospel. We have learned to associate with the people of the fallen churches of Christendom, and think in so doing we are witnessing to them. In truth, there is to be a great witness to these people, but rarely can anything productive be accomplished by joining such groups. Myriads of people are left without a witness because such ministers rarely have the courage to proselytize among the members of the churches of the other pastors. They are afraid of the reaction, should that take place. Thus many are left without a witness and are placed in circumstances which are wholly without the truth of the everlasting gospel. While we have a witness to these non-Adventist pastors, we certainly cannot join them.

Others in the United States were staggered to read that $244,000 had been budgeted for a float to participate in the Tournament of Roses parade January 1, 1992. When all around we hear of the needs of the work and the reduction in the mission budgets of five to ten percent, it seemed incredible that money could be spent on what was thought to be a witness to many people. In reality the float was seen a few fleeting moments on national television. It would be interesting to discover if even one person was drawn to the Seventh-day Adventist Church because of the witness of that float, one of hundreds that passed by the cameras during the two and one-half hours of the parade.

On the other hand, we can only speculate how many souls could be turned to the Lord had they had the opportunity of hearing the gospel because of the wise use of these funds for witnessing in countries where the gospel is still eagerly sought by men and women.

Many Seventh-day Adventists in Australia were disheartened when in 1990, two of the premier papers of the South Pacific Division, *Signs,* and *Good Health,* combined to present a special feature. Featured was Carolyn Jones, formerly a well-known presenter on Australian television who gave up that career to deliver the New Age message around the continent. Myriads of people have been drawn away from the Bible in spite of the fact that she sees Christ as her model. The *Signs/Good Health* special also publicized the radio stations presenting her messages and the times of her broadcast, *Search For Meaning.*

It is not hard to understand just how discouraged members can become by the constant failure of those with great responsibilities. It is clear that Spiritism is not just occasionally in our Adventist Church; it has flooded in like a plague. Those responsible will have a heavy account to render in the judgment.

In 1991, many of our faithful black members were startled by the New Age ingathering brochure that they were expected to use in the ingathering campaign. Perhaps more startling was the fact that many did not even see the terrible misrepresentation of God's truth in this brochure. With the desire to have something a little more contemporary, the brochure featured illustrations depicting clearly paganistic paintings. On page three a man was depicted walking upon the most ancient of pagan symbols, the shadow of the cross, to the rising sun; yet another of the ancient pagan systems. On pages eight and nine, a man in academic garb is seen kneeling toward the sun with hand raised in praise with the pagan triangles behind him. On pages twelve and thirteen the man is depicted kneeling to the rising sun with the New Age rainbow on one side and the pagan symbol of the cross on the other. Even the stylized angels, supposedly representing the three angels' messages, have the Roman Catholic halo upon their heads. It is no wonder that there were those who refused to ingather that year and that there were protests raised to those responsible. But it seems that nothing can stand in the way of the new order in the Seventh-day Adventist Church. There seems to be a determination to move in the way of Satan rather than of God.

Less noticed was the material in the 1990 issue of the appeal for missions brochure for the South Pacific Division; but there it clearly stated,

> In cooperation with governments around the world, ADRA sponsors major projects in 89 developing countries.
>
> ADRA is a member of the Australian Council For Overseas Aid (ACFOA).

This probably was less noticeable because many of those appealing for missions had no idea of the direct association of the ACFOA with the New Age movement. In a similar brochure put out by the one-world campaigners it said simply, "Join the One World campaign, under the umbrella of the Australian Council For Overseas Aid (ACFOA)." Those who chose to contribute were asked to return the contributions to "One World Campaign, Australian Council For Overseas Aid (ACFOA).

Church members want to support their leaders; they want their leaders to be models of what every church member should be. When there are so many deviations emanating from such a wide spectrum of leaders, there is an extraordinarily dangerous possibility that many will forget the faithful leaders and will categorize all leaders in the light of the actions and apostasies of those who are unfaithful.

There is an even greater danger, the danger that people will accept the aberrant direction and the apostasy of such unfaithful leaders. In so doing they will be led to eternal destruction. Surely the call of God to His leaders today is to come back to the old paths wherein is the good way, and walk therein. (Jeremiah 6:16)

> Wherefore come out from among them, and be ye separate, saith the Lord, and touch not the unclean thing; and I will receive you (2 Corinthians 6:17).

> For the wisdom of this world is foolishness with God (1 Corinthians 3:19).

19

Spiritism and Counseling

While the Bible gives us many indications of the role of counseling, never was it meant for one man's counsel to take the place of the counsel of God. The major role of any Christian counselor is to turn men and women back to the source of true counsel, the Word of God, wherein indeed is the only perfect counsel on this planet. As the years have rolled by, more and more Seventh-day Adventists have been trained in counseling. They have trained in the methodologies of the world, and in principles that are inimical to the Word of God.

In the United States it is said that there are over 200 identifiable psychological therapies, a sure indication of the fact that Satan is the author, for always Satan deals in a multiplicity of deceptions, but there can be only one true way. The Spirit of Prophecy confirms that,

> The true principles of psychology are found in the Holy Scriptures (*Mind, Character and Personality,* Volume 1, 10).

Today it is routine to train our pastors and our chaplains in counseling techniques frequently reflecting far more the principles of the world than the true principles of the Scriptures. Indeed, so pervasive has become the issue of counseling that some pastors see this as the number one responsibility of their ministry. As more pastors have gotten away from their calling as soul-winners they have become baby-sitters of the churches to which they have been appointed. Some have forsaken the counsel given by God for men not to counsel women concerning their marriage problems.

> When a woman relates her family troubles or complains of her husband to another man, she violates her marriage vows; she dishonors her husband and breaks down the wall erected to preserve the sanctity of the marriage relation; she throws wide open the door and invites Satan to enter with his insidious temptations. This is just as Satan would have it. If a woman comes to a Christian brother with a tale of her woes, her disappointments and trials, he should ever advise her, if she must confide her troubles to someone, to select sisters for

> her confidants, and then there will be no appearance of evil whereby the cause of God may suffer reproach
> *(Adventist Home,* p. 338).

In so doing these pastors have made themselves vulnerable to the appearance of evil and all too many have fallen prey to the wiles of a woman disillusioned in marriage. The two major philosophies underscoring the counseling techniques of the world have their roots in paganistic philosophy. They must be eschewed by faithful Seventh-day Adventists.

One group of therapies is built upon empiricism, the view that man has a predisposition neither to good nor to evil, and therefore is wholly the pawn of his environment. He is what he is because of the environment in which he has grown. That is a helpless view; for a poor environment would leave a man without hope in this life or in the life to come. This philosophy underscores such famous treatment modalities as behavior modification, devised by the late Professor B. F. Skinner of Harvard University.

Sister White clearly rejects this philosophy.

> It is impossible for us, of ourselves, to escape from the pit of sin in which we are sunken. Our hearts are evil, and we cannot change them. "Who can bring a clean thing out of an unclean? not one." "The carnal mind is enmity against God: for it is not subject to the law of God, neither indeed can be." Education, culture, the exercise of the will, human effort, all have their proper sphere, but here they are powerless. They may produce an outward correctness of behavior, but they cannot change the heart; they cannot purify the springs of life. There must be a power working from within, a new life from above, before men can be changed from sin to holiness
> *(Steps to Christ,* p. 18).

Just as damaging are the treatment modalities built upon the concept that man is innately good. This concept comes wholly out of the Greek pagan philosophy expounded by Socrates and other Greek philosophers. This theory holds that all you need is a good environment, and the good that is naturally in man will develop. The servant of the Lord wholly rejects this philosophy.

> The idea that it is necessary only to develop the good that exists in man by nature, is a fatal deception
> *(Steps to Christ,* pp. 18,19).

Through these pagan principles many Seventh-day Adventist psychologists, psychiatrists, counselors, and pastors are leading men in the pathway of pagan principles. As more of the philosophies of the world become overtly spiritualistic they make an impact upon those who have deeply studied into such philosophies. It cannot be surprising that we are seeing the inroads of Spiritism into our counseling. Self-centered concepts and humanistic principles often dominate.

Whereas Christianity teaches that we must accept the sinner but not the sin, pagan counseling is built upon the acceptance of both the sinner and his sin. This is consistent with the ever-advancing presentation of the sin-and-live theology abundantly common in our church today.

It is also consistent with the fact that few pastors any longer uphold, in sober tones, the mighty call of Christ, to

> Let us cleanse ourselves from all filthiness of the flesh and spirit, perfecting holiness in the fear of God
> (2 Corinthians 7:1).

Some have not been against including areas of parapsychology, hypnosis, et cetera, in such counseling situations. Some have also been drawn into such pagan practices as sensitivity groups, and we have been led into even giving demonstrations of such overtly pagan practices as levitation.

Here is an example. In a church in Texas, before an assembly of many witnesses, an Adventist chaplain sat on a chair. Around him were gathered four people, including the pastor of the church. The four placed their curled fingers on the forehead of the chaplain and all five concentrated very hard. Eventually the pastor said, "OK, now," and each of the four placed a forefinger under the chair. They lifted the chaplain until his head touched the ceiling. No human strength could have done that. The pastor made statements such as, "This just shows the power of the mind. We haven't begun to touch the power of the mind." Then they took turns in sitting in the chair as the others lifted the occupant to the ceiling. This pagan ritual was attributed to the power of the mind, when indeed it was the power of Satan.

Most tragic was the report that the children watched with wide eyes as the demonstration took place and in the following week many of them at the Adventist school associated with the church tried to repeat what they had witnessed. Eventually the teachers had to tell them to stop.

One of the most diabolical forms of counseling to which many are being introduced is regressional therapy. It is supposed that through the regressional therapy it is possible to take men and women back to their early childhood, infancy, and in some cases prenatal experiences, and there delve into the subconscious to discover the kind of painful experiences (especially emotionally painful) that are now responsible for the psychological disorders that may be manifest in the adult life of the individual. There can be no doubt that early experiences have a profound impact upon the adult life. But when we consider that Christ is able to give us victory over every hereditary and cultivated tendency to evil, surely we can trust Him to provide the power to overcome the psychological disabilities of our early life.

Commonly, regressional therapy is used to establish (in the minds of the children) incestuous relationships between parents and children. Sometimes when the patient has no recall of this, he is assured that it is deeply imbedded in his subconscious, but because of repression, he cannot recall the events. There have been a number of documented cases within the Seventh-day Adventist Church of people being convinced that when they were in childhood their parents were responsible for fearful incidents of incest.

Colin personally knows a pastor whose ministry was destroyed by such an experience. The daughter, under regressional therapy, was convinced that both her parents had sexually abused her frequently as a child, and she became so alienated and angry that she told her parents that she never wanted to see them again. She sent back every gift that she could find that the parents had ever sent to her. The impact upon the faithful ministry of this pastor and his wife was such that they were forced by the situation to take early retirement. It is to be expected that many more of these case histories will occur as more and more Seventh-day Adventists seek the counsel of those who have been trained in spiritualistic practices.

It is easy to see how readily the faithful work of a minister could be defamed and even destroyed by Satan. Of even greater concern is the fact that now some Adventist counselors are moving into direct spiritualistic practices. It is only to be expected that those who have been trained in the advanced arts of Neuro-Linguistic Programming (NLP) will seek to use some of these satanic techniques. It is possible to be led through NLP into levitation and astral projection (out of body experiences).

One such recent case in Texas illustrates vividly what is taking place. Because of the nature of the situation, the principals will not be identified, but the case involved a man who had accidently been responsible for the death of his small son. He found it so difficult to forgive himself that his family and wife decided that it was essential for him to get counseling, which he did. It was decided that this counseling should be from a Seventh-day Adventist minister so as to avoid the wrong counsel of the world. They sought advice and were given the name of a prominent minister and leader, but the counselor proved to be equally as involved in spiritualistic practice as any counselor of the world. Soon he was attempting to use such techniques as anchoring, more of which will be discussed in the chapter on "Spiritism and Neuro-Linguistic Programming."

The counselor asked the man to lie down on a couch and close his eyes, with the lights out and the blinds drawn. He was asked to imagine serene scenes such as three candles gently burning, and a scene in which he was lying on a beach with the palm trees gently waving in the breeze and the waves of the ocean rolling in. Then following spiritualistic visualization, he was asked to imagine that he was in a beautiful garden and he was asked to walk up to a large tree and look to the left. There he would see a little boy sitting with his hair gently tossed by the breeze. He was to walk up to this boy and put his arms around him. Soon it became more than imaginary as he recognized this little boy as his deceased son. As the father tried to say he was sorry, the little boy, now filled with a wisdom far beyond that of a three-year old, said to his father that he wasn't to worry, he had forgiven him. "In any case it was all in the hands of Jesus." The boy also told him that he had to say good-bye because he had to sleep for a little while and then they would see each other.

One can only imagine the emotional torment that this father went through. Here was his boy already dead but talking as if he were alive. In the counseling session, "Jesus" took the boy by the hand and walked him away. In the end, it seemed very real to this man, but by the grace of God he realized the spiritualistic nature of the counseling and refused to attend further sessions.

It seems almost unbelievable that such a pattern of counseling would be found in the Seventh-day Adventist Church, but so far have we departed from the ways of the Lord, and have turned unto paganism, that we can expect such activities to be taking place routinely in the immediate future. Surely the time has come for our pastors to fulfill the work for which God has called them, to take the message of the everlasting gospel to every nation, kindred, tongue and people and to lead men and women to the kingdom of God.

20

Spiritism and NLP (Neuro-Linguistic Programming)

In 1983 the National Association for Neuro-Linguistic Programming was founded. The basis of Neuro-Linguistic programming is riveted in the hypnosis principles of Dr. Milton Erickson. Ericksonian hypnosis claims to teach the best principles of therapeutic hypnosis. With great danger Ericksonian hypnosis teaches practitioners how to bypass the resistance of counselees by "imbedding therapeutic interventions in a seemingly casual conversation" (*The New England Institute of NLP*).

Let us look at some of the bases of this Neuro-Linguistic programming.

Magic and Hypnosis

Some recommended books for reading in Neuro-Linguistic programming are Level 1, Lewis and Pacelir, *Magic Demystified;* Level 2, Steven Langton, *Practical Magic;* Level 3, Bandler's and Grinder's, *Patterns of Hypnotic Technique,* and Grinder's and Bandler's, *Trance-formation;* Level 4, Bandler's and Grinder's *The Structure of Magic I and II*. These books alone should be sufficient warning to even half-hearted Christians that this program is not established upon God's principles. The very nature of these books orients towards paganism.

Many of the leading practitioners and teachers are skilled, trained, practicing hypnotherapists. Not only is the student trained in hypnosis, he is also trained in self-hypnosis. Of course it is argued that such hypnosis is used in an appropriate and therapeutic way by the person.

But there are many warnings against hypnosis from the servant of the Lord.

> Neither one of you should study the science [hypnosis] in which you have been interested. To study this science is to pluck the fruit from the tree of knowledge of good and evil. God forbids you or any other mortal to learn or to teach such a science
> (*Mind, Character and Personality,* Volume 2, p. 716).

> Men and women are not to study the science of how to take captive the minds of those who associate with them. This is the science that Satan teaches. We are to resist everything of the kind. We are not to tamper with mesmerism and hypnotism—the science of the one who lost his first estate and was cast out of the heavenly courts (ibid., p. 713).
>
> The theory of mind controlling mind was originated by Satan to introduce himself as the chief worker, to put human philosophy where divine philosophy should be. Of all the errors that are finding acceptance among professedly Christian people, none is a more dangerous deception, none more certain to separate man from God, than is this. Innocent though it may appear, if exercised upon patients, it will tend to their destruction, not to their restoration (ibid., p. 712).

In the Neuro-Linguistic programs, advanced hypnotic techniques used are based upon the Ericksonian model.

Deception

A second danger of Neuro-Linguistics is deception. The process of Neuro-Linguistics is designed to bypass the decision-making control of the person. Taken from one of the Neuro-Linguistic programming books, *Frogs Into Princes,* is this statement:

> If we had brought Linda up here and anchored her auditorily with voice tonalities, you'd have no idea what we did. *The more covert you are, the better off you will be* in your private practice. You can be very covert in the way you touch. You can use tones of voice. You can use words like parent, child, and adult, or postures, gestures, expressions (*Frogs Into Princes,* Richard Bandler and John Grinder, p. 102, emphasis added).

Manipulation

Associated with this deception is overt manipulation. Here is a typical example.

> Once I was lecturing to two hundred and fifty fairly astute austere psychologists, being academic, talking about representational systems and books, and drawing equations. In the middle of my academic lecture I just walked up to the edge of the stage, looked up for a moment, and said, "That's weird," then continued. A little later I looked up and did it again:

> "Well, that's really weird." I did that a couple more times during my talk, and most of the people in the first four or five rows became fixated, staring at this spot on the ceiling. Then I moved over to the side, and talked right through to them. I could get arm levitation and other unconscious responses
> (ibid., p. 91).

There is a total lack of Christian principles involved in such manipulation. Here we have deception and manipulation of the worst order. Sister White constantly warns against one mind controlling another.

> I have spoken distinctly regarding the dangerous science which says that one person shall give up his mind to the control of another. This science is the devil's own
> (*Mind, Character, and Personality,* Volume 2, p. 704).

Regarding mind control, she further said,

> Satan controls both the mind that is given up to be controlled by another and the mind that controls (ibid., p. 709).

Infallibility
There is an unbelievable claim to infallibility in the program.

> With NLP there is no failure, no resistance, no mistakes, only feedback (*NLP*, p. 3).

This program is linked with the Greek pagan idea of innate goodness. It implies the presence of the god within man which has all the solutions to his needs and his problems.

This principle is in sharp contrast with the biblical principle,

> Without me ye can do nothing (John 15:5).

Conditioning
Advocated in some of the Neuro-Linguistic programming material is the opposite principle of conditioning. You will notice this principle in the description in the following training.

> To elicit adversive responses, the therapist touches her lightly on the right shoulder. To elicit positive responses, he touches her lightly on the left shoulder. In this way it is hoped to elicit the behavior that the trainer is looking for
> (*Frogs to Princes,* p. 102).

Although we have never attended an NLP session, and have no intention of doing so, the very descriptive material available is sufficient to warn us that this training is designed by the arch-deceiver. God has the answer to the slow growth pattern of our churches. This kind of hypnotic principles could not bring men and women into the kingdom of God. They may bring people back to church attendance, but they will be pawns of the one who has hypnotized them; they will not be servants of the Lord. God has the only answer to true growth. When we are sanctified through the truth, by the Holy Spirit, we have power through the love of Christ that is greater than Pentecost, by which we attract men and women to Jesus and to His kingdom.

> Seeing ye have purified your souls in obeying the truth through the Spirit unto unfeigned love of the brethren, see that ye love one another with a pure heart fervently; being born again, not of corruptible seed, but of incorruptible, by the word of God, which liveth and abideth for ever (1 Peter 1:22–23).

New Age principles underscoring NLP are now to be found in almost every form of counseling programming, training, and development, whether it be stress control programs, marriage enrichment programs, educational enhancement programs, mind expansion programs, leadership development programs, or salesmanship training programs. But now these New Age programs have been thrust at the church in many quarters. It is assumed that, using these programs, people who were once members of the church will, through these techniques, be brought back into the empty pews. But surely, to perceptive Adventists, the way to encourage men and women back is through the loving direction of people who will present the truth in all its clarity, who will inspire these backslidden members with the power and love of God and His deep interest in their eternal salvation. No amount of the sophistries of men or human wisdom will truly bring them back into the fellowship of the Lord.

Today we have what is termed the "Calling and Caring Ministries." Nevertheless we can train people as long and hard as we like, but if their hearts are still carnal, if their motivation is still selfish, there is no salvation. We are helpless to change the state we are in and no human being, unsanctified, can be a minister to another unsanctified person and expect to see that person brought into the fellowship of Christ.

> Education, culture, the exercise of the will, human effort, all have their proper sphere, but here they are powerless. They may produce an outward correctness of behavior, but they cannot change the heart; they cannot purify the springs of life. There must be a power working from within, a new life from above, before men can be changed from sin to holiness
> *(Steps to Christ,* p. 18).

Now, literally thousands of Adventists, many of them ministers, have been trained in Lab I and, an increasing percentage of those, in Lab II. There have been hasty efforts to disassociate these programs from Neuro-Linguistic programming, but indeed they are the primary courses and the expectation is that numbers will go on into Neuro-Linguistic programs.

Dr. John Savage as the president of LEAD Consultants (Leadership, Education and Development Consultants) has indicated about five hours of NLP are to be found in Lab 1 and Lab 2. However, in a casual conversation he has pointed out that Seventh-day Adventists have a prophet who has reacted unfavorably to hypnosis, therefore it is necessary to approach Adventists a little differently, not that the elements of hypnosis are necessarily removed, but rather that the word "hypnosis," which is a pejorative term to many Seventh-day Adventists, is not used.

The denial that Lab I and Lab II courses feature Neuro-Linguistic programing is contrary to documentation. In the book *Lab I Skills for Calling and Caring Ministries* as supplied to all undertaking Lab I courses under the auspices of the South Pacific Division, on page 5 is found that one of the goals "in the area of skills" is to "Sharpen specific communication skills" in "Neuro-Linguistics."

Showing that this is no idle aim, it is found on pages 15, 16 under the heading "Skills for effective Listening" that among other things the Lab I participant will be taught:

NEURO-LINGUISTICS: Listening for & responding in the dominant mode of the speaker's language. Also, observing the speaker's eye movements for clues to the dominant mode (visual, auditory or kinesthetic) (ibid., pp. 15, 16).

The entire page 44a is devoted to Neuro-Linguistic programming. At the conclusion of the book the list of suggested readings for Lab I is headed by "Bandler, Richard and Grinder, John, *Frogs Into Princes: Neuro-Linguistic Programming.* Utah: Real People Press, 1979."

To deny that Neuro-Linguistic programming is being taught to our Seventh-day Adventist pastors and laypeople in the Lab I courses is to deny irrefutable documentation. Such denials only increase the concerns of God's people. When the editor of the *Adventist Review* comes out in defense of Lab I and Lab II courses and states that

> NLP in itself is not a sinister concept
> (*Adventist Review,* February 20, 1992),

further alarm bells ring. The *Adventist Review* editor states that his replies came from a North American Division study of these programs which will later be published in *Ministry* magazine.

Further, the editor answers the question "Does Lab I teach NLP therapy?" with an emphatic "No." Of course, this is an instance of the proverbial case of asking the wrong question and thus providing an answer which is designed to calm the fears of the readers. The correct question should have been, "Do Lab I courses utilize the principles of NLP?" A truthful answer to that question would arouse our people to deep concern.

The effects of this article were multiplied by its reproduction in the *South Pacific Record* (April 4, 1992). When Bro. C. R. Bennett of New Zealand wrote a letter of concern to the editor (ibid., May 2, 1992), the editor responded in the same issue by stating

> We're also concerned about a one-sided view. So concerned, in fact, that henceforth we'll only consider publishing correspondence on this topic from those who have, and state that they have, attended Lab I (ibid).

Such a decision smacks not of concern that a one-sided view will be presented but rather of a ploy to ensure that the "debate" *will* be one sided. Unless an individual is prepared to study Lab I, with the very real danger that his perceptions will be altered, not by the Holy Spirit, but the spiritualistic methods invoked, then he is banned from taking part in the discussion. Apparently documentation is not valued, perhaps because it would present a very different picture from that of those who have studied a course based upon a system designed to alter the judgment and minds of individuals.

Few studying this course appear to be aware of the fact that Richard Bandler, who with John Grinder created Neuro-Linguistic programming, was prone to excessive alcohol intake and addicted to cocaine. He was also charged with murder. (*Mother Jones,* The Bandler Method, Feb./March 1989, pp. 24-28, 63, 64, by Frank Clancy and Heidi Yorkshire.) This is the type of mind from which this "harmless" program has been derived. The entire genesis of NLP is satanic.

That God's church would support a program steeped in this type of material is beyond comprehension. If only we were as apt to defend the Biblical evidence on the human nature of Christ and other salient doctrines under attack, as we are to rise up in defense of NLP and Celebration services, how different our church would be. If care is not taken, we could well reach a stage where the words and programs of worldlings are more valued that the words and programs of Scripture.

Because Lab 1 commences with what is a very low-key presentation on listening skills, many are not initially able to see the humanistic nature of the training, especially as it has been modified to present its philosophy within the program of reclaiming inactive members. We do not question the need for our members to be out seeking those who have left the Seventh-day Adventist Church; this is most necessary. But it will become a natural response to true conversion. Any man or woman who has truly the love and power of Christ is impelled to witness.

Peter and John said,

> For we cannot but speak the things which we have seen and heard (Acts 4:20).

There is an impelling motivation that comes from the indwelling love of Jesus. Men and women seek to reach out to the lost with the love that Jesus had when He gave His life for them. Many of our members are now frightened; frightened that they will be hypnotized unwittingly by trained pastor-counselors. Their fear is not unjustified in some cases.

Some see this training as leading to deceptive practices by the same pastors. For example, if a member perceives that the pastor has preached error in the sermon and approaches the pastor to discuss the matter, the pastor may soon distract him by asking a question quite irrelevant to their conversation. The pastor then moves into a direction that does not permit the person to come back to the topic of his deep concern. More Seventh-day Adventists, recognizing that their pastors have had such training, are deciding to find churches where the pastor has not had such training, and if that is impossible in the area, they are opting for home churches on Sabbath. This is a pitiful situation but one that is understandable, for it would be totally out of harmony with God's counsel to continue to listen to someone who is under the hypnotic control of Satan.

All these situations give evidence to the fact that the faithful who are giving the warning call are referred to as the troublers of Israel, the critics of the church and of leadership, but it is surely those who are following in the pathway of Satan who are responsible for the terrible division in the church. We should not be surprised, for the Lord has warned that there would be wheat and tares, sheep and goats, gold and dross. God will harvest in the faithful and the rest will be bound together for eternal destruction. The tragedy is that the majority of Seventh-day Adventists will be lost in the testing time ahead. Our burden as authors is that everyone reading this book will take a decided stand for truth and righteousness, and away from the deceptions of Satan, and will become active participants in helping others to find God's way and His salvation.

21

The Way of Christ or the Way of the World

There is no secret concerning the reason Spiritism has made such rapid inroads into our beloved church in recent years. We have now permitted the world to enter the church on a grand scale. When we wish to promote church growth we go to the world for its counsel. We go to the world to learn how to worship. We go to the world to learn how to counsel others. We go to the world to discover how to promote cell meetings. We are guided by the world in order to understand theology and prepare to teach it. We seek the world's training to win the backslidden. We are enchanted by the world's methods of retaining our youth. Frequently we adopt worldly standards in our medical institutions. Many turn to the world for scientific understanding. We often trust the thoughts of worldly theologians and educators in preference to the inspired counsel of the prophet. We are increasingly promoting a worldly standard in our church entertainments. For many, worldly music is acceptable. Our Adventist Book Centers are increasingly turning to the sale of fiction and other materials based upon the reading materials of the world. These are not one whit better than many historical novels. Our magazines, especially for the youth, are apeing the world. Ministers even go to the world for fraternal fellowship.

With these and many other documented facts, is it any wonder that the acme of worldliness—Spiritism—has found a fertile breeding ground in the Seventh-day Adventist Church?

There is one solution—a return to the Word of God. We are no longer, in general, a people of the Book. We have educated ourselves away from God's counsels and have lusted for the "wisdom" of the world. The results, predictable in their immensity, have proven to have had a devastating impact upon God's holy Church. Our Saviour is and ever will be,

> Wonderful, Counsellor, The mighty God, The everlasting Father, The Prince of Peace   (Isaiah 9:6).

Thus the final decision of all mankind is identical to man's first decision; whether we accept the Word of God, the One who is the Truth and cannot lie, or accept the word of Satan, the one who is the father of lies. The decision will be whether to follow the pure, unadulterated truth of the Word of God, or to accept one of the myriad philosophies of the arch-deceiver, Satan.

As we have explored some of the satanic deceptions of Spiritism in the Seventh-day Adventist Church, we can assure you that we have only touched the tip of the iceberg. There is much more material that we could have presented and probably we have been made aware of only a very small part of the evidence. But certainly we can see the effectiveness of Satan's determined effort to destroy the true church that was to arise at the end of time—a church that was built on the commandments of God and the faith of Jesus, that would be called of God to take the everlasting gospel to every nation and kindred and tongue and people.

When Sister White wrote the *The Great Controversy,* she indicated that Satan had not yet reached the full development of his plans. Today he must be very close to reaching that fulfillment.

> Satan has long been preparing for his final effort to deceive the world. . . . Little by little he has prepared the way for his masterpiece of deception in the development of Spiritualism. He has not yet reached the full accomplishment of his designs; but it will be reached in the last remnant of time
>
> (*The Great Controversy,* p. 561).

We also cannot but point out the error. Though there may be some who would say that this book has been a criticism of the church, that would be a total misrepresentation. It has been a rebuke to all those who would bring aberrant spiritualist principles into the Seventh-day Adventist Church, no matter how high or low their position. Like the warriors of old we have no alternative. Sister White puts it this way:

> In every generation God has sent His servants to rebuke sin, both in the world and in the church. But the people desire smooth things spoken to them, and the pure, unvarnished truth is not acceptable. Many reformers, in entering upon their work, determined to exercise great prudence in attacking

> the sins of the church and the nation. They hoped, by the example of a pure Christian life, to lead the people back to the doctrines of the Bible. But the Spirit of God came upon them as it came upon Elijah, moving him to rebuke the sins of a wicked king and an apostate people; they could not refrain from preaching the plain utterances of the Bible—doctrines which they had been reluctant to present. They were impelled to zealously declare the truth, and the danger which threatened souls. The words which the Lord gave them they uttered, fearless of consequences, and the people were compelled to hear the warning (*The Great Controversy,* p. 606).

We pray that every reader of this book will be compelled to hear the warning, and what is more important, that each will heed the warning. We pray that if in any way you have been participants in any of the inroads of Spiritism, either wittingly or unwittingly, with prayer and confession you will turn from these wicked ways and will become stalwarts in standing firm and secure for God's truth and His righteousness. We pray that others who have remained silent will now, under the unction of the Holy Spirit, stand up and speak out, for their silence is surely the worst kind of neutrality in this time of terrible crisis within God's church. The protests need to rise in a deafening crescendo so that even the most Laodicean slumberer will be aroused and will have to make a decision for the Lord or against Him. Only then can we see the fullness of the proclamation of the third angel's message.

> Thus the message of the third angel will be proclaimed. As the time comes for it to be given with greatest power, the Lord will work through humble instruments, leading the minds of those who consecrate themselves to His service. The laborers will be qualified rather by the unction of His spirit than by the training of literary institutions. Men of faith and prayer will be constrained to go forth with holy zeal, declaring the words which God gives them. The sins of Babylon will be laid open. The fearful results of enforcing the observances of the church by civil authority, the inroads of Spiritualism, the stealthy but rapid progress of papal power—all will be unmasked. By these solemn warnings the people will be stirred. Thousands upon thousands will listen who have never heard words like these (ibid.).

We must not be deceived by men and women of high position in the church if they are following the dictates of Satan. God's servant warned concerning some of the leaders of the Jews,

> The same evil spirit that tempted Christ in the wilderness, and that possessed the maniac of Capernaum, controlled the unbelieving Jews. But with them he assumed an air of piety, seeking to deceive them as to their motives in rejecting the Saviour. Their condition was more hopeless than that of the demoniac, for they felt no need of Christ and were therefore held fast under the power of Satan
>
> (*The Desire of Ages*, p. 256).

It may be pastors and leaders who in reading this book will come under deep conviction that they have not been following the pathway of Christ and that they have indeed been following the pathway of Satan. Now is the time for such pastors to not only repent, but also to do everything they can to repair the terrible damage they have done to God's flock.

Recognize that we should have been fully prepared for what we are seeing in our beloved church today. But for most of us, no matter how well we have been warned by the Bible and Spirit of Prophecy, it has still come as a fearful shock. The servant of the Lord gave us this kind of warning in dealing with the holy flesh movement:

> Last January the Lord showed me that erroneous theories and methods would be brought into our camp meetings, and that the history of the past would be repeated. I felt greatly distressed. I was instructed to say that at these demonstrations demons in the form of men are present, working with all the ingenuity that Satan can employ to make the truth disgusting to sensible people; that the enemy was trying to arrange matters so that the camp meetings, which have been the means of bringing the truth of the third angel's message before multitudes, should lose their force and influence.
>
> The third angel's message is to be given in straight lines. It is to be kept free from every thread of the cheap, miserable inventions of men's theories, prepared by the father of lies, and disguised as was the brilliant serpent used by Satan as a medium for deceiving our first parents. Thus Satan tried to put his stamp upon the work God would have stand forth in purity.

The Holy Spirit has nothing to do with such a confusion of noise and multitude of sounds as passed before me last January. Satan works amid the din and confusion of such music, which, properly conducted, would be a praise and glory to God. He makes its effect like the poison sting of the serpent.

Those things which have been in the past will be in the future. Satan will make music a snare by the way in which it is conducted. God calls upon His people, who have the light before them in the Word and in the Testimonies, to read and consider, and to take heed. Clear and definite instruction has been given in order that all may understand. But the itching desire to originate something new results in strange doctrines, and largely destroys the influence of those who would be a power for good if they held firm the beginning of their confidence in the truth that the Lord had given them
(Selected Messages, Volume 2, pp. 37–38).

We must cut loose from every deception of Satan. We must not move a step away from the great truths that God has given to us. These are the mighty closing moments of earth's history. This is the time when Satan is moving "as a roaring lion seeking whom he may devour." This is the time that he is going to the length and breadth of the earth with nearly irresistible deceptions, yet we need not be deceived if we place our life fully in the hands of Christ. If every morning we plead with Him to preserve us from yielding to temptation and from being deceived, He will not let us down. If every morning we commit our heart and life to His sacred Word, we cannot fail. For only those "who have fortified the mind with the truths of the Bible will stand through the last great conflict" *(The Great Controversy,* pp. 593, 594).

This is the time to stand under the blood-stained banner of Jesus Christ. This is the time to lift up that banner, when many are allowing it to trail in the dust, and raise it high. This is the time to stand when champions are few. This is the time to be as true to principle as the needle is to the pole. This is the time to have

The courage of heroes and the faith of martyrs
(Testimonies for the Church, vol. 5, p. 187).